THE DAILY READING BIBLE

Volume 18

ACTS 1-9   NUMBERS   COLOSSIANS

The Daily Reading Bible (Volume 18)
© Matthias Media 2009

Matthias Media
(St Matthias Press Ltd ACN 067 558 365)
PO Box 225
Kingsford NSW 2032
Australia
Ph: (02) 9663 1478; Int. +61-2-9663-1478
Fax: (02) 9663 3265; Int. +61-2-9663-3265
Email: info@matthiasmedia.com.au
Internet: www.matthiasmedia.com.au

Matthias Media (USA)
Ph: 724 964 8152; Int. +1-724-964-8152
Fax: 724 964 8166; Int. +1-724-964-8166
Email: sales@matthiasmedia.com
Internet: www.matthiasmedia.com

All Scripture is taken from the Holy Bible, English Standard Version, copyright © 2001 by Crossway Bibles, a publishing ministry of Good News Publishers. Used by permission. All rights reserved.

ISBN 978 1 921441 36 3

All rights reserved. Except as may be permitted by the Copyright Act, no part of this publication may be reproduced in any form or by any means without prior permission from the publisher.

Cover design and typesetting by Matthias Media.
Series concept design by www.madebydesign.com.au

CONTENTS

Introduction — **Page 5**

Acts 1-9 — **Page 7**

Numbers — **Page 29**

Colossians — **Page 55**

Appendix — **Page 71**

INTRODUCTION

Reading our Bibles regularly is getting harder. That, at least, seems to be the common experience of many Christians. We could waste lots of ink speculating on the reasons for this: is it the frenetic pace of life these days? Is it spiritual laziness? Is it the impact of postmodernism on our culture and the lack of certainty when it comes to interpreting the written word?

But a better option than speculating on the reasons, we thought, was to provide a new resource for Christians to help them get back into a more regular habit of reflecting daily on God's word. So back in June 2001, we decided to start including a section called 'Bible Brief' in our monthly magazine, *The Briefing* (see www.matthiasmedia.com.au for more information about *The Briefing*). The 'Bible Brief' provided 20 short readings each month—acknowledging that there will be days we miss or days when we want to do something a bit different—with questions, thoughts to ponder, and suggestions to get started in prayer.

Now, several years later, we have a good collection of 'Bible Briefs', and it's time to offer them to a wider audience in a format that will, we hope, be even more convenient and useful.

This eighteenth volume contains 60 readings, all designed to be done in 15-20 minutes. These daily Bible readings are designed to help you feed regularly from God's word. They won't cover every issue in each passage, nor even every passage from each Bible book. In other words, *they are no substitute for the in-depth study of the Scriptures* that you may undertake personally, in small groups or through listening to sermons.

With the kind permission of our friends at Crossway Bibles, we've been able to make this a complete package to take with you—we've included the English Standard Version Bible text with each daily study. So you can take this one book with you and have everything you need—on the train, on the bus, or to the park at lunchtime—wherever and whenever you can get 20 minutes to yourself.

How to use these readings

- *With a penitent heart*, the true prerequisite for all Bible reading. Open with prayer (perhaps using the prayer suggested at the beginning of each set of studies).
- *With 15-20 minutes* of peace and quiet. If you can take longer, and want to read and pray further—great! But we have designed the readings to be done in a fairly short space of time.
- *With an accurate modern translation*. We recommend and have included the new ESV translation. The writers of the studies refer to this translation. Contact us for further details about the ESV or visit www.matthiasmedia.com.au/ESV

- *With a pen.* Even if you only jot down brief ideas, writing focuses the mind.
- *As a guide and help, not a straitjacket.* Feel free to dig further into the passage, to notice and ponder things that the questions don't point to.
- *As a launch-pad for prayer.* Use the prayer ideas at the end of each reading as a starting point for your daily prayer. Many of the points that will arise from the readings will be things you can pray for yourself, and also for others (family, friends, neighbours, etc.). Why not compile a list of people you want to pray for (you can write them in the blank space below), and use the prayer ideas from each reading to pray for the next person on your list?

This eighteenth volume includes:
- studies on Acts 1-9 (written by Bryson Smith, one of the members of the ministry team at Dubbo Presbyterian Church)
- studies on Numbers (written by Simon Flinders, assistant minister at St Thomas' Anglican Church, North Sydney)
- studies on Colossians (written by Neil Atwood, associate pastor at Springwood/ Winmalee Anglican Church).

Matthias Media
April 2009

Please note: the main section of Scripture for each study is reproduced before the questions. Other Scripture references are reproduced as footnotes at the bottom of the page, or, where the passages are too long to be included as footnotes, in the appendix.

PEOPLE TO PRAY FOR:

ACTS 1-9

INTRODUCTION

Do you ever wish you were part of something big? Every day the alarm goes off in the morning, you roll out of bed for another day and go through the same old routine. Everything seems so mundane and small-scale. Do you sometimes feel like it would be nice to be caught up in something a bit more spectacular?

The book of Acts is a wonderful book because it helps us to see that when we are followers of Jesus, we are, in fact, caught up in something much bigger than ourselves. As Christians, we are caught up in a worldwide movement—a passing on of a message that has been transforming people's lives in every single country on the face of this earth for thousands of years. We share the thrill of being labourers in the ongoing, outgoing work of the risen Christ!

You might like to use this prayer (or your own variation of it) before each of the next 20 studies:

Dear God and Father,
Thank you for your compassion and mercy in allowing me to call you my Father. Thank you for saving me in these last days through the grace of the Lord Jesus Christ. Thank you in the name of Jesus Christ for granting me forgiveness for my sins and the gift of the Holy Spirit. As I read your word in Acts, please continue your good work in me. Please transform me so that I will think your thoughts and share your passions. Dear Father, please change me so that I will be your effective and productive servant.
Amen.

NB: Tick the box when you've completed each study ✓

READING 1 — ACTS 1:1-11

In the first book, O Theophilus, I have dealt with all that Jesus began to do and teach, ² until the day when he was taken up, after he had given commands through the Holy Spirit to the apostles whom he had chosen. ³ He presented himself alive to them after his suffering by many proofs, appearing to them during forty days and speaking about the kingdom of God.

⁴ And while staying with them he ordered them not to depart from Jerusalem, but to wait for the promise of the Father, which, he said, "you heard from me; ⁵ for John baptized with water, but you will be baptized with the Holy Spirit not many days from now."

⁶ So when they had come together, they asked him, "Lord, will you at this time restore the kingdom to Israel?" ⁷ He said to them, "It is not for you to know times or seasons that the Father has fixed by his own authority. ⁸ But you will receive power when the Holy Spirit has come upon you, and you will be my

witnesses in Jerusalem and in all Judea and Samaria, and to the end of the earth." 9 And when he had said these things, as they were looking on, he was lifted up, and a cloud took him out of their sight. 10 And while they were gazing into heaven as he went, behold, two men stood by them in white robes, 11 and said, "Men of Galilee, why do you stand looking into heaven? This Jesus, who was taken up from you into heaven, will come in the same way as you saw him go into heaven."

1. What does the phrase "all that Jesus began to do and teach" (v. 1) lead you to expect about the book of Acts?

2. What special plans does Jesus have for his disciples?

3. What signs are there in the passage that indicate that the disciples don't yet understand Jesus' plans and purposes?

PONDER What are the implications (if any) for you of Jesus' instructions to his disciples?

PRAYER IDEAS Thank God for the ongoing work of Jesus Christ in this world. Thank him in particular for the gift of his Holy Spirit.

READING 2 — ACTS 1:12-26

Then they returned to Jerusalem from the mount called Olivet, which is near Jerusalem, a Sabbath day's journey away. 13 And when they had entered, they went up to the upper room, where they were staying, Peter and John and James and Andrew, Philip and Thomas, Bartholomew and Matthew, James the son of Alphaeus and Simon the Zealot and Judas the son of James. 14 All these with one accord were devoting themselves to prayer, together with the women and Mary the mother of Jesus, and his brothers.

15 In those days Peter stood up among the brothers (the company of persons was in all about 120) and said, 16 "Brothers, the Scripture had to be fulfilled, which the Holy Spirit spoke beforehand by the mouth of David concerning Judas, who became a guide to those who arrested Jesus. 17 For he was numbered among us and was allotted his share in this ministry." 18 (Now this man acquired a field with the reward of his wickedness, and falling headlong he burst open in the middle and all his bowels gushed out. 19 And it became known to all the inhabitants of Jerusalem, so that the field was called in their own language Akeldama, that is, Field of Blood.) 20 "For it is written in the Book of Psalms,

"'May his camp become desolate,
 and let there be no one to dwell in it';

and

"'Let another take his office.'

21 So one of the men who have accompanied us during all the time that the Lord Jesus went in and out among us, 22 beginning from the baptism of John until the day when he was taken up from us—one of these men must become with us a witness to his resurrection." 23 And they put forward two, Joseph called Barsabbas, who was also called Justus, and Matthias. 24 And they prayed and said, "You,

Lord, who know the hearts of all, show which one of these two you have chosen [25] to take the place in this ministry and apostleship from which Judas turned aside to go to his own place." [26] And they cast lots for them, and the lot fell on Matthias, and he was numbered with the eleven apostles.

1. What happened to Judas?

2. Peter quotes Psalms 69:25[1] and 109:8[2] — both psalms of David in which David calls upon God to judge his enemies. Where do you see the fulfilment of these Scriptures in Judas' fate?

3. What characteristics must Judas' replacement have?

4. According to verses 24-25, why did the disciples cast lots?

PONDER Do you think it's ever okay to toss a coin in order to pick a Christian leader?

PRAYER IDEAS Thank God for the way in which the message of the gospel has been protected throughout history by faithful witnesses of Jesus.

READING 3   ACTS 2:1-21

When the day of Pentecost arrived, they were all together in one place. [2] And suddenly there came from heaven a sound like a mighty rushing wind, and it filled the entire house where they were sitting. [3] And divided tongues as of fire appeared to them and rested on each one of them. [4] And they were all filled with the Holy Spirit and began to speak in other tongues as the Spirit gave them utterance.

[5] Now there were dwelling in Jerusalem Jews, devout men from every nation under heaven. [6] And at this sound the multitude came together, and they were bewildered, because each one was hearing them speak in his own language. [7] And they were amazed and astonished, saying, "Are not all these who are speaking Galileans? [8] And how is it that we hear, each of us in his own native language? [9] Parthians and Medes and Elamites and residents of Mesopotamia, Judea and Cappadocia, Pontus and Asia, [10] Phrygia and Pamphylia, Egypt and the parts of Libya belonging to Cyrene, and visitors from Rome, [11] both Jews and proselytes, Cretans and Arabians—we hear them telling in our own tongues the mighty works of God." [12] And all were amazed and perplexed, saying to one another, "What does this mean?" [13] But others mocking said, "They are filled with new wine."

[14] But Peter, standing with the eleven, lifted up his voice and addressed them: "Men of Judea and all who dwell in Jerusalem, let this be known to you, and give ear to my words. [15] For these people are not drunk, as you suppose, since it is only the third hour of the day. [16] But this is what was uttered through the prophet Joel:

---

1. May their camp be a desolation; let no one dwell in their tents.
2. May his days be few; may another take his office!

THE DAILY READING BIBLE VOLUME 18

PONDER If Jesus really is both Lord and Christ, how should you treat him?

PRAYER IDEAS Think over verse 33 and use it as a basis for prayer.

READING 5 — ACTS 2:37-47

Now when they heard this they were cut to the heart, and said to Peter and the rest of the apostles, "Brothers, what shall we do?" 38 And Peter said to them, "Repent and be baptized every one of you in the name of Jesus Christ for the forgiveness of your sins, and you will receive the gift of the Holy Spirit. 39 For the promise is for you and for your children and for all who are far off, everyone whom the Lord our God calls to himself." 40 And with many other words he bore witness and continued to exhort them, saying, "Save yourselves from this crooked generation." 41 So those who received his word were baptized, and there were added that day about three thousand souls.

42 And they devoted themselves to the apostles' teaching and the fellowship, to the breaking of bread and the prayers. 43 And awe came upon every soul, and many wonders and signs were being done through the apostles. 44 And all who believed were together and had all things in common. 45 And they were selling their possessions and belongings and distributing the proceeds to all, as any had need. 46 And day by day, attending the temple together and breaking bread in their homes, they received their food with glad and generous hearts, 47 praising God and having favor with all the people. And the Lord added to their number day by day those who were being saved.

1. How do the crowds react to the news that Jesus, whom they crucified, is in fact Lord and Christ?

2. What does Peter say they should do and why?

3. What characteristics do the new believers have?

PONDER In verse 40, Peter 'bears witness' and 'continues to exhort them'. What makes his message so urgent? Do you share this urgency?

PRAYER IDEAS Think of a person you know who needs to hear the gospel. Ask God for boldness, wisdom, sensitivity and the opportunity to bear witness to them and exhort them.

READING 6 — ACTS 3:1-10

Now Peter and John were going up to the temple at the hour of prayer, the ninth hour. 2 And a man lame from birth was being carried, whom they laid daily at the gate of the temple that is called the Beautiful Gate to ask alms of those entering the temple. 3 Seeing Peter and John about to go into the temple, he asked to receive alms. 4 And Peter directed his gaze at him, as did John, and said, "Look at us." 5 And he fixed his attention on them, expecting to receive something from them. 6 But Peter said, "I have no silver and gold, but what I do have I give to you. In the name of Jesus Christ of Nazareth, rise up and walk!" ⁷ And he took him by the right hand and raised him up, and immediately his feet and ankles were made strong. ⁸ And leaping up he stood and began to walk, and entered the temple with them, walking and leaping and praising God. ⁹ And all the people saw him walking and praising God, ¹⁰ and recognized him as the one who sat at the Beautiful Gate of the temple, asking for alms. And they were filled with wonder and amazement at what had happened to him.

1. What are you told about the beggar? (See also pointer below.)

2. How does the beggar react to his healing? (Note where he goes.) How do the crowds react?

3. How is this miracle a picture of the gospel?

PONDER In Acts, when people receive blessing through Jesus Christ, it is always associated with rejoicing and praising. To what extent does rejoicing and praising God characterize your lifestyle?

PRAYER IDEAS Thank God for making you clean like the beggar through the power of Jesus' name.

POINTER v. 2: It's significant that the beggar begged *outside* the temple. This reflects his ceremonial 'uncleanness': being lame, he was not permitted to enter.

READING 7 — ACTS 3:11-26

While he clung to Peter and John, all the people, utterly astounded, ran together to them in the portico called Solomon's. ¹² And when Peter saw it he addressed the people: "Men of Israel, why do you wonder at this, or why do you stare at us, as though by our own power or piety we have made him walk? ¹³ The God of Abraham, the God of Isaac, and the God of Jacob, the God of our fathers, glorified his servant Jesus, whom you delivered over and denied in the presence of Pilate, when he had decided to release him. ¹⁴ But you denied the Holy and Righteous One, and asked for a murderer to be granted to you, ¹⁵ and you killed the Author of life, whom God raised from the dead. To this we are witnesses. ¹⁶ And his name—by faith in his name—has made this man strong whom you see and know, and the faith that is through Jesus has given the man this perfect health in the presence of you all.

¹⁷ "And now, brothers, I know that you acted in ignorance, as did also your rulers. ¹⁸ But what God foretold by the mouth of all the prophets, that his Christ would suffer, he thus fulfilled. ¹⁹ Repent therefore, and turn again, that your sins may be blotted out, ²⁰ that times of refreshing may come from the presence of the Lord, and that he may send the Christ appointed for you, Jesus, ²¹ whom heaven must receive until the time for restoring all the things about which God spoke by the mouth of his holy prophets long ago. ²² Moses said, 'The Lord God will raise up for you a prophet like me from your brothers. You shall listen to him in whatever he tells you. ²³ And it shall be that every soul who does not listen to that prophet shall

be destroyed from the people.' ²⁴ And all the prophets who have spoken, from Samuel and those who came after him, also proclaimed these days. ²⁵ You are the sons of the prophets and of the covenant that God made with your fathers, saying to Abraham, 'And in your offspring shall all the families of the earth be blessed.' ²⁶ God, having raised up his servant, sent him to you first, to bless you by turning every one of you from your wickedness."

1. According to Peter, how was the beggar healed?

2. What does Peter say the crowd should do? Why? (Note the similarities to what Peter said in 2:38-39.³)

3. What are the consequences of not responding to Jesus in the right way?

PONDER Peter explained to the crowd that the followers of Jesus have had their sins "blotted out". What difference should this make to the way you relate to God and treat others?

PRAYER IDEAS Ask God to help you and other Christians you know to persevere and hold on to your faith until "the time for restoring all the things about which God spoke by the mouth of his holy prophets long ago" (v. 21).

READING 8 — ACTS 4:1-22

And as they were speaking to the people, the priests and the captain of the temple and the Sadducees came upon them, ² greatly annoyed because they were teaching the people and proclaiming in Jesus the resurrection from the dead. ³ And they arrested them and put them in custody until the next day, for it was already evening. ⁴ But many of those who had heard the word believed, and the number of the men came to about five thousand.

⁵ On the next day their rulers and elders and scribes gathered together in Jerusalem, ⁶ with Annas the high priest and Caiaphas and John and Alexander, and all who were of the high-priestly family. ⁷ And when they had set them in the midst, they inquired, "By what power or by what name did you do this?" ⁸ Then Peter, filled with the Holy Spirit, said to them, "Rulers of the people and elders, ⁹ if we are being examined today concerning a good deed done to a crippled man, by what means this man has been healed, ¹⁰ let it be known to all of you and to all the people of Israel that by the name of Jesus Christ of Nazareth, whom you crucified, whom God raised from the dead—by him this man is standing before you well. ¹¹ This Jesus is the stone that was rejected by you, the builders, which has become the cornerstone. ¹² And there is salvation in no one else, for there is no other name under heaven given among men by which we must be saved."

¹³ Now when they saw the boldness of Peter

---

3. And Peter said to them, "Repent and be baptized every one of you in the name of Jesus Christ for the forgiveness of your sins, and you will receive the gift of the Holy Spirit. ³⁹ For the promise is for you and for your children and for all who are far off, everyone whom the Lord our God calls to himself."

and John, and perceived that they were uneducated, common men, they were astonished. And they recognized that they had been with Jesus. ¹⁴ But seeing the man who was healed standing beside them, they had nothing to say in opposition. ¹⁵ But when they had commanded them to leave the council, they conferred with one another, ¹⁶ saying, "What shall we do with these men? For that a notable sign has been performed through them is evident to all the inhabitants of Jerusalem, and we cannot deny it. ¹⁷ But in order that it may spread no further among the people, let us warn them to speak no more to anyone in this name." ¹⁸ So they called them and charged them not to speak or teach at all in the name of Jesus. ¹⁹ But Peter and John answered them, "Whether it is right in the sight of God to listen to you rather than to God, you must judge, ²⁰ for we cannot but speak of what we have seen and heard." ²¹ And when they had further threatened them, they let them go, finding no way to punish them, because of the people, for all were praising God for what had happened. ²² For the man on whom this sign of healing was performed was more than forty years old.

1. Why are Peter and John suddenly in trouble?

2. How do Peter and John react?

3. List all the things you discover about Jesus in this passage.

PONDER "And there is salvation in no one else, for there is no other name under heaven given among men by which we must be saved" (v. 12). Why is this such an unpopular message?

PRAYER IDEAS In a world that prides itself on tolerance and the acceptance of all religions, ask God for the courage to obey him instead of men.

READING 9 — ACTS 4:23-31

When they were released, they went to their friends and reported what the chief priests and the elders had said to them. ²⁴ And when they heard it, they lifted their voices together to God and said, "Sovereign Lord, who made the heaven and the earth and the sea and everything in them, ²⁵ who through the mouth of our father David, your servant, said by the Holy Spirit,

"'Why did the Gentiles rage,
  and the peoples plot in vain?
²⁶ The kings of the earth set themselves,
  and the rulers were gathered together,
    against the Lord and against his
      Anointed'—

²⁷ for truly in this city there were gathered together against your holy servant Jesus, whom you anointed, both Herod and Pontius Pilate, along with the Gentiles and the peoples of Israel, ²⁸ to do whatever your hand and your plan had predestined to take place. ²⁹ And now, Lord, look upon their threats and grant to your servants to continue to speak your word with all boldness, ³⁰ while you stretch out your hand to heal, and signs and wonders are performed through the name of your holy servant Jesus." ³¹ And when they had prayed, the place in which they were gathered together was shaken, and they were all filled with the Holy Spirit and continued to speak the word of God with boldness.

1. After their release, the disciples quote Psalm 2. Read the psalm through for yourself (see the appendix, p. 71)—it's a beauty! Why would this psalm have been particularly comforting to the disciples?

2. What do the disciples ask for specifically in 4:29? How is their prayer answered in verse 31?

PONDER Why are you, at times, not as bold about Jesus as you should be?

PRAYER IDEAS Use Psalm 2 as a basis for prayer. In particular, thank God for the refuge you have in Christ.

READING 10 — ACTS 4:32-5:11

Now the full number of those who believed were of one heart and soul, and no one said that any of the things that belonged to him was his own, but they had everything in common. 33 And with great power the apostles were giving their testimony to the resurrection of the Lord Jesus, and great grace was upon them all. 34 There was not a needy person among them, for as many as were owners of lands or houses sold them and brought the proceeds of what was sold 35 and laid it at the apostles' feet, and it was distributed to each as any had need. 36 Thus Joseph, who was also called by the apostles Barnabas (which means son of encouragement), a Levite, a native of Cyprus, 37 sold a field that belonged to him and brought the money and laid it at the apostles' feet.

5:1 But a man named Ananias, with his wife Sapphira, sold a piece of property, 2 and with his wife's knowledge he kept back for himself some of the proceeds and brought only a part of it and laid it at the apostles' feet. 3 But Peter said, "Ananias, why has Satan filled your heart to lie to the Holy Spirit and to keep back for yourself part of the proceeds of the land? 4 While it remained unsold, did it not remain your own? And after it was sold, was it not at your disposal? Why is it that you have contrived this deed in your heart? You have not lied to men but to God." 5 When Ananias heard these words, he fell down and breathed his last. And great fear came upon all who heard of it. 6 The young men rose and wrapped him up and carried him out and buried him.

7 After an interval of about three hours his wife came in, not knowing what had happened. 8 And Peter said to her, "Tell me whether you sold the land for so much." And she said, "Yes, for so much." 9 But Peter said to her, "How is it that you have agreed together to test the Spirit of the Lord? Behold, the feet of those who have buried your husband are at the door, and they will carry you out." 10 Immediately she fell down at his feet and breathed her last. When the young men came in they found her dead, and they carried her out and buried her beside her husband. 11 And great fear came upon the whole church and upon all who heard of these things.

1. How were the believers caring for one another?

2. What was Ananias and Sapphira's sin?

3. Peter speaks of Ananias' lying to the church as if he was lying to God (5:4). How does this illustrate the fact that the church is precious to the risen Christ? How might this explain the "great fear" that seized the church (v. 11)?

PONDER What is the appropriate way for you to exercise "fear" in the way you treat your church family?

PRAYER IDEAS Ask God to help you to recognize the preciousness of his household. Ask him to grant you creative generosity as you serve others in your church family.

READING 11 — ACTS 5:12-28

Now many signs and wonders were regularly done among the people by the hands of the apostles. And they were all together in Solomon's Portico. 13 None of the rest dared join them, but the people held them in high esteem. 14 And more than ever believers were added to the Lord, multitudes of both men and women, 15 so that they even carried out the sick into the streets and laid them on cots and mats, that as Peter came by at least his shadow might fall on some of them. 16 The people also gathered from the towns around Jerusalem, bringing the sick and those afflicted with unclean spirits, and they were all healed.

17 But the high priest rose up, and all who were with him (that is, the party of the Sadducees), and filled with jealousy 18 they arrested the apostles and put them in the public prison. 19 But during the night an angel of the Lord opened the prison doors and brought them out, and said, 20 "Go and stand in the temple and speak to the people all the words of this Life." 21 And when they heard this, they entered the temple at daybreak and began to teach.

Now when the high priest came, and those who were with him, they called together the council and all the senate of the people of Israel and sent to the prison to have them brought. 22 But when the officers came, they did not find them in the prison, so they returned and reported, 23 "We found the prison securely locked and the guards standing at the doors, but when we opened them we found no one inside." 24 Now when the captain of the temple and the chief priests heard these words, they were greatly perplexed about them, wondering what this would come to. 25 And someone came and told them, "Look! The men whom you put in prison are standing in the temple and teaching the people." 26 Then the captain with the officers went and brought them, but not by force, for they were afraid of being stoned by the people.

27 And when they had brought them, they set them before the council. And the high priest questioned them, 28 saying, "We strictly charged you not to teach in this name, yet here you have filled Jerusalem with your teaching, and you intend to bring this man's blood upon us."

1. Why are the disciples in trouble this time?

2. How do you think the disciples felt when they re-entered the temple in verse 21?

3. How does this passage demonstrate Jesus' determination to have his gospel preached in Jerusalem? How does this fit into Jesus' mission plan in Acts 1:8?[4] (See especially verse 28.)

PONDER So far, we have seen the work of the risen Christ opposed for theological reasons (4:1-2[5]), as well as because of crass jealousy (v. 17). In your experience, why else is Christianity criticized and opposed?

PRAYER IDEAS Ask God to give you boldness so that you will witness about Jesus, even when it might cause trouble for you.

READING 12 — ACTS 5:29-42

But Peter and the apostles answered, "We must obey God rather than men. 30 The God of our fathers raised Jesus, whom you killed by hanging him on a tree. 31 God exalted him at his right hand as Leader and Savior, to give repentance to Israel and forgiveness of sins. 32 And we are witnesses to these things, and so is the Holy Spirit, whom God has given to those who obey him."

33 When they heard this, they were enraged and wanted to kill them. 34 But a Pharisee in the council named Gamaliel, a teacher of the law held in honor by all the people, stood up and gave orders to put the men outside for a little while. 35 And he said to them, "Men of Israel, take care what you are about to do with these men. 36 For before these days Theudas rose up, claiming to be somebody, and a number of men, about four hundred, joined him. He was killed, and all who followed him were dispersed and came to nothing. 37 After him Judas the Galilean rose up in the days of the census and drew away some of the people after him. He too perished, and all who followed him were scattered. 38 So in the present case I tell you, keep away from these men and let them alone, for if this plan or this undertaking is of man, it will fail; 39 but if it is of God, you will not be able to overthrow them. You might even be found opposing God!" So they took his advice, 40 and when they had called in the apostles, they beat them and charged them not to speak in the name of Jesus, and let them go. 41 Then they left the presence of the council, rejoicing that they were counted worthy to suffer dishonor for the name. 42 And every day, in the temple and from house to house, they did not cease teaching and preaching Jesus as the Christ.

1. How has the hostility against the disciples escalated in this passage? (Compare verses 33 and 40 with 5:17-18[6] and 4:1-3,[7] 18-21.[8])

---

4. "But you will receive power when the Holy Spirit has come upon you, and you will be my witnesses in Jerusalem and in all Judea and Samaria, and to the end of the earth."
5. And as they were speaking to the people, the priests and the captain of the temple and the Sadducees came upon them, [2] greatly annoyed because they were teaching the people and proclaiming in Jesus the resurrection from the dead.
6. But the high priest rose up, and all who were with him (that is, the party of the Sadducees), and filled with jealousy 18 they arrested the apostles and put them in the public prison.
7. And as they were speaking to the people, the priests and the captain of the temple and the Sadducees came upon them,

[2] greatly annoyed because they were teaching the people and proclaiming in Jesus the resurrection from the dead. 3 And they arrested them and put them in custody until the next day, for it was already evening.
8. So they called them and charged them not to speak or teach at all in the name of Jesus. 19 But Peter and John answered them, "Whether it is right in the sight of God to listen to you rather than to God, you must judge, 20 for we cannot but speak of what we have seen and heard." 21 And when they had further threatened them, they let them go, finding no way to punish them, because of the people, for all were praising God for what had happened.

2. What do you discover about Jesus from Peter's speech?

3. What is Gamaliel's argument? What do you think of it?

PONDER What does it mean to be "counted worthy to suffer dishonor for the name" (v. 41)? How is it possible to rejoice in this?

PRAYER IDEAS Meditate over verse 29 and use it as a basis for prayer.

READING 13 — ACTS 6:1-7

Now in these days when the disciples were increasing in number, a complaint by the Hellenists arose against the Hebrews because their widows were being neglected in the daily distribution. ² And the twelve summoned the full number of the disciples and said, "It is not right that we should give up preaching the word of God to serve tables. ³ Therefore, brothers, pick out from among you seven men of good repute, full of the Spirit and of wisdom, whom we will appoint to this duty. ⁴ But we will devote ourselves to prayer and to the ministry of the word." ⁵ And what they said pleased the whole gathering, and they chose Stephen, a man full of faith and of the Holy Spirit, and Philip, and Prochorus, and Nicanor, and Timon, and Parmenas, and Nicolaus, a proselyte of Antioch. ⁶ These they set before the apostles, and they prayed and laid their hands on them.

⁷ And the word of God continued to increase, and the number of the disciples multiplied greatly in Jerusalem, and a great many of the priests became obedient to the faith.

1. What complaint do the Hellenists make? How serious an issue do you think this is?

2. According to verses 1-2, what is in danger of happening as a result of this complaint?

3. What solution do the apostles arrive at? Do you think it's a good solution? Why?

PONDER In this passage, the disciples are in danger of becoming diverted from the task to which God had called them. How are you susceptible to the same danger? What sort of 'good' things can divert you from the 'best' things in following the risen Christ?

PRAYER IDEAS Ask God to "fulfill every resolve for good and every work of faith by his power" (2 Thess 1:11b).

POINTER v. 1: The Hellenists were Greek-speaking Jews.

READING 14

ACTS 6:8-7:29

And Stephen, full of grace and power, was doing great wonders and signs among the people. 9 Then some of those who belonged to the synagogue of the Freedmen (as it was called), and of the Cyrenians, and of the Alexandrians, and of those from Cilicia and Asia, rose up and disputed with Stephen. 10 But they could not withstand the wisdom and the Spirit with which he was speaking. 11 Then they secretly instigated men who said, "We have heard him speak blasphemous words against Moses and God." 12 And they stirred up the people and the elders and the scribes, and they came upon him and seized him and brought him before the council, 13 and they set up false witnesses who said, "This man never ceases to speak words against this holy place and the law, 14 for we have heard him say that this Jesus of Nazareth will destroy this place and will change the customs that Moses delivered to us." 15 And gazing at him, all who sat in the council saw that his face was like the face of an angel.

7:1 And the high priest said, "Are these things so?" 2 And Stephen said:

"Brothers and fathers, hear me. The God of glory appeared to our father Abraham when he was in Mesopotamia, before he lived in Haran, 3 and said to him, 'Go out from your land and from your kindred and go into the land that I will show you.' 4 Then he went out from the land of the Chaldeans and lived in Haran. And after his father died, God removed him from there into this land in which you are now living. 5 Yet he gave him no inheritance in it, not even a foot's length, but promised to give it to him as a possession and to his offspring after him, though he had no child. 6 And God spoke to this effect—that his offspring would be sojourners in a land belonging to others, who would enslave them and afflict them four hundred years. 7 'But I will judge the nation that they serve,' said God, 'and after that they shall come out and worship me in this place.' 8 And he gave him the covenant of circumcision. And so Abraham became the father of Isaac, and circumcised him on the eighth day, and Isaac became the father of Jacob, and Jacob of the twelve patriarchs.

9 "And the patriarchs, jealous of Joseph, sold him into Egypt; but God was with him 10 and rescued him out of all his afflictions and gave him favor and wisdom before Pharaoh, king of Egypt, who made him ruler over Egypt and over all his household. 11 Now there came a famine throughout all Egypt and Canaan, and great affliction, and our fathers could find no food. 12 But when Jacob heard that there was grain in Egypt, he sent out our fathers on their first visit. 13 And on the second visit Joseph made himself known to his brothers, and Joseph's family became known to Pharaoh. 14 And Joseph sent and summoned Jacob his father and all his kindred, seventy-five persons in all. 15 And Jacob went down into Egypt, and he died, he and our fathers, 16 and they were carried back to Shechem and laid in the tomb that Abraham had bought for a sum of silver from the sons of Hamor in Shechem.

17 "But as the time of the promise drew near, which God had granted to Abraham, the people increased and multiplied in Egypt 18 until there arose over Egypt another king who did not know Joseph. 19 He dealt shrewdly with our race and forced our fathers to expose their infants, so that they would not be kept alive. 20 At this time Moses was born; and he was beautiful in God's sight. And he was brought up for three months in his father's house, 21 and when he was exposed, Pharaoh's daughter adopted him and brought him up as her own son. 22 And Moses was instructed in all the wisdom of the Egyptians, and he was mighty in his words and deeds.

²³ "When he was forty years old, it came into his heart to visit his brothers, the children of Israel. ²⁴ And seeing one of them being wronged, he defended the oppressed man and avenged him by striking down the Egyptian. ²⁵ He supposed that his brothers would understand that God was giving them salvation by his hand, but they did not understand. ²⁶ And on the following day he appeared to them as they were quarreling and tried to reconcile them, saying, 'Men, you are brothers. Why do you wrong each other?' ²⁷ But the man who was wronging his neighbor thrust him aside, saying, 'Who made you a ruler and a judge over us? ²⁸ Do you want to kill me as you killed the Egyptian yesterday?' ²⁹ At this retort Moses fled and became an exile in the land of Midian, where he became the father of two sons."

1. What complaints are made against Stephen?

2. Why do you think Stephen recounts so much of the Old Testament in his speech?

PONDER How is God's faithfulness to his promises to Abraham relevant to you? (If you have time, read Galatians 3:7-29 in the appendix.)

PRAYER IDEAS Thank God for revealing himself throughout history, and for showing himself to be reliable and faithful.

READING 15 — ACTS 7:30-8:1

In this reading, we rejoin Stephen's speech as he defends himself before the Sanhedrin.

"Now when forty years had passed, an angel appeared to him in the wilderness of Mount Sinai, in a flame of fire in a bush. ³¹ When Moses saw it, he was amazed at the sight, and as he drew near to look, there came the voice of the Lord: ³² 'I am the God of your fathers, the God of Abraham and of Isaac and of Jacob.' And Moses trembled and did not dare to look. ³³ Then the Lord said to him, 'Take off the sandals from your feet, for the place where you are standing is holy ground. ³⁴ I have surely seen the affliction of my people who are in Egypt, and have heard their groaning, and I have come down to deliver them. And now come, I will send you to Egypt.'

³⁵ "This Moses, whom they rejected, saying, 'Who made you a ruler and a judge?'—this man God sent as both ruler and redeemer by the hand of the angel who appeared to him in the bush. ³⁶ This man led them out, performing wonders and signs in Egypt and at the Red Sea and in the wilderness for forty years. ³⁷ This is the Moses who said to the Israelites, 'God will raise up for you a prophet like me from your brothers.' ³⁸ This is the one who was in the congregation in the wilderness with the angel who spoke to him at Mount Sinai, and with our fathers. He received living oracles to give to us. ³⁹ Our fathers refused to obey him, but thrust him aside, and in their hearts they turned to Egypt, ⁴⁰ saying to Aaron, 'Make for us gods who will go before us. As for this Moses who led us out from the land of Egypt, we do not know what has become of him.' ⁴¹ And they made a calf in those days, and offered a sacrifice to the idol and were rejoicing in the works of their hands. ⁴² But God turned away and gave them over to worship the host of heaven, as it is written in the book of the prophets:

"'Did you bring to me slain beasts and sacrifices,
during the forty years in the wilderness, O house of Israel?
⁴³ You took up the tent of Moloch
and the star of your god Rephan,
the images that you made to worship;
and I will send you into exile beyond Babylon.'

⁴⁴ "Our fathers had the tent of witness in the wilderness, just as he who spoke to Moses directed him to make it, according to the pattern that he had seen. ⁴⁵ Our fathers in turn brought it in with Joshua when they dispossessed the nations that God drove out before our fathers. So it was until the days of David, ⁴⁶ who found favor in the sight of God and asked to find a dwelling place for the God of Jacob. ⁴⁷ But it was Solomon who built a house for him. ⁴⁸ Yet the Most High does not dwell in houses made by hands, as the prophet says,

⁴⁹ "'Heaven is my throne,
and the earth is my footstool.
What kind of house will you build for me, says the Lord,
or what is the place of my rest?
⁵⁰ Did not my hand make all these things?'

⁵¹ "You stiff-necked people, uncircumcised in heart and ears, you always resist the Holy Spirit. As your fathers did, so do you. ⁵² Which of the prophets did your fathers not persecute? And they killed those who announced beforehand the coming of the Righteous One, whom you have now betrayed and murdered, ⁵³ you who received the law as delivered by angels and did not keep it."

⁵⁴ Now when they heard these things they were enraged, and they ground their teeth at him. ⁵⁵ But he, full of the Holy Spirit, gazed into heaven and saw the glory of God, and Jesus standing at the right hand of God. ⁵⁶ And he said, "Behold, I see the heavens opened, and the Son of Man standing at the right hand of God." ⁵⁷ But they cried out with a loud voice and stopped their ears and rushed together at him. ⁵⁸ Then they cast him out of the city and stoned him. And the witnesses laid down their garments at the feet of a young man named Saul. ⁵⁹ And as they were stoning Stephen, he called out, "Lord Jesus, receive my spirit." ⁶⁰ And falling to his knees he cried out with a loud voice, "Lord, do not hold this sin against them." And when he had said this, he fell asleep.

8:1 And Saul approved of his execution.

And there arose on that day a great persecution against the church in Jerusalem, and they were all scattered throughout the regions of Judea and Samaria, except the apostles.

1. *Stephen was accused of being against the temple. What does Stephen say about the temple in 7:44-50? How is his response a defence against these accusations?*

2. *Stephen was accused of being against Moses. What does Stephen say about Moses in 7:35-39? How is his response a defence against these accusations?*

3. *What finally happens to Stephen? How does this make you feel?*

PONDER How is Stephen a good example for you to follow?

PRAYER IDEAS Do you know of someone experiencing real hardship because of their faith? Ask God to bless them with endurance and perseverance.

READING 16 — ACTS 8:1-25

And Saul approved of his execution. And there arose on that day a great persecution against the church in Jerusalem, and they were all scattered throughout the regions of Judea and Samaria, except the apostles. 2 Devout men buried Stephen and made great lamentation over him. 3 But Saul was ravaging the church, and entering house after house, he dragged off men and women and committed them to prison.

4 Now those who were scattered went about preaching the word. 5 Philip went down to the city of Samaria and proclaimed to them the Christ. 6 And the crowds with one accord paid attention to what was being said by Philip when they heard him and saw the signs that he did. 7 For unclean spirits, crying out with a loud voice, came out of many who had them, and many who were paralyzed or lame were healed. 8 So there was much joy in that city.

9 But there was a man named Simon, who had previously practiced magic in the city and amazed the people of Samaria, saying that he himself was somebody great. 10 They all paid attention to him, from the least to the greatest, saying, "This man is the power of God that is called Great." 11 And they paid attention to him because for a long time he had amazed them with his magic. 12 But when they believed Philip as he preached good news about the kingdom of God and the name of Jesus Christ, they were baptized, both men and women. 13 Even Simon himself believed, and after being baptized he continued with Philip. And seeing signs and great miracles performed, he was amazed.

14 Now when the apostles at Jerusalem heard that Samaria had received the word of God, they sent to them Peter and John, 15 who came down and prayed for them that they might receive the Holy Spirit, 16 for he had not yet fallen on any of them, but they had only been baptized in the name of the Lord Jesus. 17 Then they laid their hands on them and they received the Holy Spirit. 18 Now when Simon saw that the Spirit was given through the laying on of the apostles' hands, he offered them money, 19 saying, "Give me this power also, so that anyone on whom I lay my hands may receive the Holy Spirit." 20 But Peter said to him, "May your silver perish with you, because you thought you could obtain the gift of God with money! 21 You have neither part nor lot in this matter, for your heart is not right before God. 22 Repent, therefore, of this wickedness of yours, and pray to the Lord that, if possible, the intent of your heart may be forgiven you. 23 For I see that you are in the gall of bitterness and in the bond of iniquity." 24 And Simon answered, "Pray for me to the Lord, that nothing of what you have said may come upon me."

25 Now when they had testified and spoken the word of the Lord, they returned to Jerusalem, preaching the gospel to many villages of the Samaritans.

1. What negative things resulted from the death of Stephen?

2. What positive thing resulted from the death of Stephen?

3. What is the significance of verses 1 and 4 in light of what Jesus said in 1:8?[9]

4. In verses 15-16, why do you think the Holy Spirit had not come upon any of the people prior to the arrival of Peter and John?

PONDER With the persecution that arises after Stephen's death, God takes a bad situation and uses it for his own purposes. Such is his determination to spread the gospel. Where in your own life has God also done this?

PRAYER IDEAS This section marks a decisive moment in Jesus' mission plan: the gospel has now gone to the Samaritans! Thank God for the fact that the risen Christ wants all people to be saved. Ask him to place this desire in your heart as well.

READING 17   ACTS 8:26-40

Now an angel of the Lord said to Philip, "Rise and go toward the south to the road that goes down from Jerusalem to Gaza." This is a desert place. 27 And he rose and went. And there was an Ethiopian, a eunuch, a court official of Candace, queen of the Ethiopians, who was in charge of all her treasure. He had come to Jerusalem to worship 28 and was returning, seated in his chariot, and he was reading the prophet Isaiah. 29 And the Spirit said to Philip, "Go over and join this chariot." 30 So Philip ran to him and heard him reading Isaiah the prophet and asked, "Do you understand what you are reading?" 31 And he said, "How can I, unless someone guides me?" And he invited Philip to come up and sit with him. 32 Now the passage of the Scripture that he was reading was this:

"Like a sheep he was led to the slaughter and like a lamb before its shearer is silent,
so he opens not his mouth.
33 In his humiliation justice was denied him.
   Who can describe his generation?
For his life is taken away from the earth."

34 And the eunuch said to Philip, "About whom, I ask you, does the prophet say this, about himself or about someone else?" 35 Then Philip opened his mouth, and beginning with this Scripture he told him the good news about Jesus. 36 And as they were going along the road they came to some water, and the eunuch said, "See, here is water! What prevents me from being baptized?"* 38 And he commanded the chariot to stop, and they both went down into the water, Philip and the eunuch, and he baptized him. 39 And when they came up out of the

---

9. "But you will receive power when the Holy Spirit has come upon you, and you will be my witnesses in Jerusalem and in all Judea and Samaria, and to the end of the earth."

* Some manuscripts add all or most of verse 37: *And Philip said, "If you believe with all your heart, you may." And he replied, "I believe that Jesus Christ is the Son of God."*

water, the Spirit of the Lord carried Philip away, and the eunuch saw him no more, and went on his way rejoicing. ⁴⁰ But Philip found himself at Azotus, and as he passed through he preached the gospel to all the towns until he came to Caesarea.

1. Who does Philip tell the gospel to this time? What do you find out about this person?

2. Why do you think Luke singles out this event in his narrative?

3. What do you learn about the risen Christ from what Philip tells the eunuch?

PONDER Why do you think Luke wrote "the Spirit of the Lord carried Philip away" (v. 39)? What does this tell you about who is in control of all these events?

PRAYER IDEAS Re-read verses 32-33 and use them as a basis for thanking God for Christ.

READING 18   ACTS 9:1-19

But Saul, still breathing threats and murder against the disciples of the Lord, went to the high priest ² and asked him for letters to the synagogues at Damascus, so that if he found any belonging to the Way, men or women, he might bring them bound to Jerusalem. ³ Now as he went on his way, he approached Damascus, and suddenly a light from heaven flashed around him. ⁴ And falling to the ground he heard a voice saying to him, "Saul, Saul, why are you persecuting me?" ⁵ And he said, "Who are you, Lord?" And he said, "I am Jesus, whom you are persecuting. ⁶ But rise and enter the city, and you will be told what you are to do." ⁷ The men who were traveling with him stood speechless, hearing the voice but seeing no one. ⁸ Saul rose from the ground, and although his eyes were opened, he saw nothing. So they led him by the hand and brought him into Damascus. ⁹ And for three days he was without sight, and neither ate nor drank.

¹⁰ Now there was a disciple at Damascus named Ananias. The Lord said to him in a vision, "Ananias." And he said, "Here I am, Lord." ¹¹ And the Lord said to him, "Rise and go to the street called Straight, and at the house of Judas look for a man of Tarsus named Saul, for behold, he is praying, ¹² and he has seen in a vision a man named Ananias come in and lay his hands on him so that he might regain his sight." ¹³ But Ananias answered, "Lord, I have heard from many about this man, how much evil he has done to your saints at Jerusalem. ¹⁴ And here he has authority from the chief priests to bind all who call on your name." ¹⁵ But the Lord said to him, "Go, for he is a chosen instrument of

mine to carry my name before the Gentiles and kings and the children of Israel. ¹⁶ For I will show him how much he must suffer for the sake of my name." ¹⁷ So Ananias departed and entered the house. And laying his hands on him he said, "Brother Saul, the Lord Jesus who appeared to you on the road by which you came has sent me so that you may regain your sight and be filled with the Holy Spirit." ¹⁸ And immediately something like scales fell from his eyes, and he regained his sight. Then he rose and was baptized; ¹⁹ and taking food, he was strengthened.

For some days he was with the disciples at Damascus.

1. What sort of person is Saul at the beginning of this passage?

2. What sort of person is Saul by the end of the passage?

3. What is Christ's plan for Saul?

PONDER "If God can forgive Saul, he can forgive anyone!" Do you think that's true? Are there times when you limit God's grace? Why?

PRAYER IDEAS Read 1 Corinthians 15:1-11 (see the appendix, p. 72) and use it as a basis for prayer.

READING 19 — ACTS 9:20-30

And immediately he proclaimed Jesus in the synagogues, saying, "He is the Son of God." ²¹ And all who heard him were amazed and said, "Is not this the man who made havoc in Jerusalem of those who called upon this name? And has he not come here for this purpose, to bring them bound before the chief priests?" ²² But Saul increased all the more in strength, and confounded the Jews who lived in Damascus by proving that Jesus was the Christ.

²³ When many days had passed, the Jews plotted to kill him, ²⁴ but their plot became known to Saul. They were watching the gates day and night in order to kill him, ²⁵ but his disciples took him by night and let him down through an opening in the wall, lowering him in a basket.

²⁶ And when he had come to Jerusalem, he attempted to join the disciples. And they were all afraid of him, for they did not believe that he was a disciple. ²⁷ But Barnabas took him and brought him to the apostles and declared to them how on the road he had seen the Lord, who spoke to him, and how at Damascus he had preached boldly in the name of Jesus. ²⁸ So he went in and out among them at Jerusalem, preaching boldly in the name of the Lord. ²⁹ And he spoke and disputed against the Hellenists. But they were seeking to kill him. ³⁰ And when the brothers learned this, they brought him down to Caesarea and sent him off to Tarsus.

1. It's ironic that the man who used to kill Christians is now in danger of being killed himself (vv. 23-24, 29). How does this demonstrate the power of the risen Christ?

2. How does Barnabas live up to his name in these verses? (See 4:36.[10])

PONDER What exactly has caused such a big change in Saul? What lesson do you learn from this?

PRAYER IDEAS Read Galatians 1:11-24 (see the appendix, p. 72) and use it as a basis for prayer.

READING 20 — ACTS 9:31

So the church throughout all Judea and Galilee and Samaria had peace and was being built up. And walking in the fear of the Lord and in the comfort of the Holy Spirit, it multiplied.

1. What makes this verse a good summary of the book so far—especially in terms of Jesus' mission plan for the world? (See 1:8.[11])

2. What are some of the different ways you have seen the church being strengthened and encouraged by the Holy Spirit throughout the book of Acts?

3. What does it mean to be "walking in the fear of the Lord"?

PONDER Skim back over the chapters you have covered in Acts. Is there a particular passage that has challenged or comforted you? What made it challenging/comforting?

PRAYER IDEAS Spend some time thanking God for those people whom the risen Christ has used to bring the gospel to you. Ask God to use you to take that gospel to others.

---

10. Thus Joseph, who was also called by the apostles Barnabas (which means son of encouragement), a Levite, a native of Cyprus ...

11. "But you will receive power when the Holy Spirit has come upon you, and you will be my witnesses in Jerusalem and in all Judea and Samaria, and to the end of the earth."

NUMBERS

INTRODUCTION

The book of Numbers describes the period when Israel wandered in the wilderness—the time between their departure from Egypt when God rescued them from Pharaoh (see the book of Exodus) and their entry into the Promised Land (see the book of Joshua). It's really the story of two generations—the generation of Israelites who left Egypt in the exodus but never entered the Promised Land, and the generation who went in and took possession of the land. Numbers tells us why it was the second rather than the first that entered the land. The book gets its name because it is structured around two censuses (or 'numberings'), one for each generation (see chapters 1 and 26).

You might like to use this prayer (or your own variation of it) before each of the next 20 studies:

Father,
Please bless me as I read your word. May your gracious face shine upon me. Deepen my appreciation for all you have done. Strengthen me to obey all you have said. Please keep me in your kingdom and give me peace. In Jesus' name,
Amen.

READING 21 — NUMBERS 1:1-19, 44-45, 54; 2:34

PLOT SUMMARY *Chapter 1 describes the first census of Israel that God asked Moses to take (soon after they left Egypt—see 1:1), and chapter 2 describes the formation in which the Israelite tribes were to both camp and travel on their journey.*

Numbers 1:1-19

The LORD spoke to Moses in the wilderness of Sinai, in the tent of meeting, on the first day of the second month, in the second year after they had come out of the land of Egypt, saying, [2] "Take a census of all the congregation of the people of Israel, by clans, by fathers' houses, according to the number of names, every male, head by head. [3] From twenty years old and upward, all in Israel who are able to go to war, you and Aaron shall list them, company by company. [4] And there shall be with you a man from each tribe, each man being the head of the house of his fathers. [5] And these are the names of the men who shall assist you. From Reuben, Elizur the son of Shedeur; [6] from Simeon, Shelumiel the son of Zurishaddai; [7] from Judah, Nahshon the son of Amminadab; [8] from Issachar, Nethanel the son of Zuar; [9] from Zebulun, Eliab the son of Helon; [10] from the sons of Joseph, from Ephraim, Elishama the son of Ammihud, and from Manasseh, Gamaliel the son of Pedahzur; [11] from Benjamin, Abidan the son of Gideoni; [12] from Dan, Ahiezer the son of Ammishaddai; [13] from Asher, Pagiel the son of Ochran; [14] from Gad, Eliasaph the son of Deuel; [15] from Naphtali, Ahira the son of Enan." [16] These were the ones chosen from the congregation, the chiefs of their ancestral tribes, the heads of the clans of Israel.

[17] Moses and Aaron took these men who had been named, [18] and on the first day of the second month, they assembled the whole congregation together, who registered themselves by clans, by fathers' houses, according to the number of names from twenty years old and upward, head by head, [19] as the Lord commanded Moses. So he listed them in the wilderness of Sinai.

Numbers 1:44-45

These are those who were listed, whom Moses and Aaron listed with the help of the chiefs of Israel, twelve men, each representing his fathers' house. [45] So all those listed of the people of Israel, by their fathers' houses, from twenty years old and upward, every man able to go to war in Israel ...

Numbers 1:54

Thus did the people of Israel; they did according to all that the Lord commanded Moses.

Numbers 2:34

Thus did the people of Israel. According to all that the Lord commanded Moses, so they camped by their standards, and so they set out, each one in his clan, according to his fathers' house.

1. Whom did God want to be counted in the census?

2. Did the Israelites do what God wanted?

PONDER Israel's obedience to God in these chapters is a picture of what Israel should have been. This picture will end up being an indictment against Israel when they are disobedient. What is your assessment of your own obedience/disobedience to God?

PRAYER IDEAS Read 1 Peter 1:14[12] and acknowledge God as the one who demands and deserves your obedience. Ask him to strengthen you to be an obedient child.

READING 22   NUMBERS 3:1-16

PLOT SUMMARY *Chapters 3-4 are concerned with Moses' counting of the priests within Israel and God's instructions about their particular duties with respect to the tent of meeting (or tabernacle).*

These are the generations of Aaron and Moses at the time when the Lord spoke with Moses on Mount Sinai. [2] These are the names of the sons of Aaron: Nadab the firstborn, and Abihu, Eleazar, and Ithamar. [3] These are the names of the sons of Aaron, the anointed priests, whom he ordained to serve as priests. [4] But Nadab and Abihu died before the Lord when they offered unauthorized fire before the Lord in the wilderness of Sinai, and they had no children. So Eleazar and Ithamar served as priests in

---

[12]. As obedient children, do not be conformed to the passions of your former ignorance ...

the lifetime of Aaron their father.

⁵ And the LORD spoke to Moses, saying, ⁶ "Bring the tribe of Levi near, and set them before Aaron the priest, that they may minister to him. ⁷ They shall keep guard over him and over the whole congregation before the tent of meeting, as they minister at the tabernacle. ⁸ They shall guard all the furnishings of the tent of meeting, and keep guard over the people of Israel as they minister at the tabernacle. ⁹ And you shall give the Levites to Aaron and his sons; they are wholly given to him from among the people of Israel. ¹⁰ And you shall appoint Aaron and his sons, and they shall guard their priesthood. But if any outsider comes near, he shall be put to death."

¹¹ And the LORD spoke to Moses, saying, ¹² "Behold, I have taken the Levites from among the people of Israel instead of every firstborn who opens the womb among the people of Israel. The Levites shall be mine, ¹³ for all the firstborn are mine. On the day that I struck down all the firstborn in the land of Egypt, I consecrated for my own all the firstborn in Israel, both of man and of beast. They shall be mine: I am the LORD."

¹⁴ And the LORD spoke to Moses in the wilderness of Sinai, saying, ¹⁵ "List the sons of Levi, by fathers' houses and by clans; every male from a month old and upward you shall list." ¹⁶ So Moses listed them according to the word of the LORD, as he was commanded.

1. Who were given a role as priests within Israel? Who were to minister to the priests?

2. What were their responsibilities?

3. Why did the firstborn of every Israelite belong to God (vv. 11-13)? (See Exodus 13:1-2¹³ and the story of Exodus 12 in the appendix.)

PONDER What does the warning in verse 10 tell you about the nature of the tabernacle, the importance of the priests' work and the character of God?

PRAYER IDEAS Read Hebrews 9:11-12.¹⁴ Thank God for sending Jesus to enter the heavenly "tent" (or tabernacle) for you, and for redeeming you by Jesus' blood so that you can now approach him without fear of death.

READING 23

NUMBERS 5:1-4, 6:1-12

PLOT SUMMARY Chapters 5-6 contain laws God gave to preserve the purity of the Israelite camp and its people. Chapter 6 finishes with a blessing that the priests were to say.

Numbers 5:1-4

The LORD spoke to Moses, saying, ² "Command the people of Israel that they put out of the camp everyone who is leprous or has a discharge and everyone who is unclean through contact with the dead. ³ You shall

---

13. The LORD said to Moses, ² "Consecrate to me all the firstborn. Whatever is the first to open the womb among the people of Israel, both of man and of beast, is mine."
14. But when Christ appeared as a high priest of the good things that have come, then through the greater and more perfect tent (not made with hands, that is, not of this creation) ¹² he entered once for all into the holy places, not by means of the blood of goats and calves but by means of his own blood, thus securing an eternal redemption.

put out both male and female, putting them outside the camp, that they may not defile their camp, in the midst of which I dwell." ⁴ And the people of Israel did so, and put them outside the camp; as the Lord said to Moses, so the people of Israel did.

Numbers 6:1-12

And the Lord spoke to Moses, saying, ² "Speak to the people of Israel and say to them, When either a man or a woman makes a special vow, the vow of a Nazirite, to separate himself to the Lord, ³ he shall separate himself from wine and strong drink. He shall drink no vinegar made from wine or strong drink and shall not drink any juice of grapes or eat grapes, fresh or dried. ⁴ All the days of his separation he shall eat nothing that is produced by the grapevine, not even the seeds or the skins.

⁵ "All the days of his vow of separation, no razor shall touch his head. Until the time is completed for which he separates himself to the Lord, he shall be holy. He shall let the locks of hair of his head grow long.

⁶ "All the days that he separates himself to the Lord he shall not go near a dead body. ⁷ Not Lord for his father or for his mother, for brother or sister, if they die, shall he make himself unclean, because his separation to God is on his head. ⁸ All the days of his separation he is holy to the Lord.

⁹ "And if any man dies very suddenly beside him and he defiles his consecrated head, then he shall shave his head on the day of his cleansing; on the seventh day he shall shave it. ¹⁰ On the eighth day he shall bring two turtledoves or two pigeons to the priest to the entrance of the tent of meeting, ¹¹ and the priest shall offer one for a sin offering and the other for a burnt offering, and make atonement for him, because he sinned by reason of the dead body. And he shall consecrate his head that same day ¹² and separate himself to the Lord for the days of his separation and bring a male lamb a year old for a guilt offering. But the previous period shall be void, because his separation was defiled.

1. In 5:3, what reason was given for the importance of the camp's purity?

2. Notice in 6:11 that impurity for the Nazirite is described as 'sin'. What needed to happen when the Nazirite sinned?

PONDER Read 1 John 1:8-2:2.[15] How is the way sin is dealt with in this passage different to what is prescribed in Numbers?

PRAYER IDEAS Thank God for the cleansing he offers you through the sacrifice of Jesus. Confess your sins to God. Praise him for his forgiveness.

POINTER As you read through Numbers, you will notice that it moves between 'laws' and 'narrative' (story) quite regularly. Remember that the laws were very important to the Israelites: they outlined how God wanted them to live.

---

[15]. If we say we have no sin, we deceive ourselves, and the truth is not in us. ⁹ If we confess our sins, he is faithful and just to forgive us our sins and to cleanse us from all unrighteousness. ¹⁰ If we say we have not sinned, we make him a liar, and his word is not in us.

2:1 My little children, I am writing these things to you so that you may not sin. But if anyone does sin, we have an advocate with the Father, Jesus Christ the righteous. ² He is the propitiation for our sins, and not for ours only but also for the sins of the whole world.

READING 24

NUMBERS 8:5-19

PLOT SUMMARY *Chapter 7 describes the offerings that were made when the tabernacle was dedicated. Chapter 8 contains God's instructions for the tabernacle's lamps, and for the service of the Levites in the tabernacle.*

And the LORD spoke to Moses, saying, [6] "Take the Levites from among the people of Israel and cleanse them. [7] Thus you shall do to them to cleanse them: sprinkle the water of purification upon them, and let them go with a razor over all their body, and wash their clothes and cleanse themselves. [8] Then let them take a bull from the herd and its grain offering of fine flour mixed with oil, and you shall take another bull from the herd for a sin offering. [9] And you shall bring the Levites before the tent of meeting and assemble the whole congregation of the people of Israel. [10] When you bring the Levites before the LORD, the people of Israel shall lay their hands on the Levites, [11] and Aaron shall offer the Levites before the LORD as a wave offering from the people of Israel, that they may do the service of the LORD. [12] Then the Levites shall lay their hands on the heads of the bulls, and you shall offer the one for a sin offering and the other for a burnt offering to the LORD to make atonement for the Levites. [13] And you shall set the Levites before Aaron and his sons, and shall offer them as a wave offering to the LORD.

[14] "Thus you shall separate the Levites from among the people of Israel, and the Levites shall be mine. [15] And after that the Levites shall go in to serve at the tent of meeting, when you have cleansed them and offered them as a wave offering. [16] For they are wholly given to me from among the people of Israel. Instead of all who open the womb, the firstborn of all the people of Israel, I have taken them for myself. [17] For all the firstborn among the people of Israel are mine, both of man and of beast. On the day that I struck down all the firstborn in the land of Egypt I consecrated them for myself, [18] and I have taken the Levites instead of all the firstborn among the people of Israel. [19] And I have given the Levites as a gift to Aaron and his sons from among the people of Israel, to do the service for the people of Israel at the tent of meeting and to make atonement for the people of Israel, that there may be no plague among the people of Israel when the people of Israel come near the sanctuary."

1. What does this passage tell you about the work the Levites would have to do in the tabernacle?

2. Why do you think the Levites needed to be cleansed/purified before they could serve in the tabernacle?

3. What was involved in cleansing/purifying the Levites?

PONDER Read Hebrews 7:26-27.[16] What does this passage tell you about Jesus and the nature of his service? How does he compare with the Levites?

---

[16] For it was indeed fitting that we should have such a high priest, holy, innocent, unstained, separated from sinners, and exalted above the heavens. [27] He [i.e. Jesus] has no need, like those high priests, to offer sacrifices daily, first for his own sins and then for those of the people, since he did this once for all when he offered up himself.

PRAYER IDEAS Praise God for Jesus' perfect life and perfect death. Thank him humbly for Jesus' priestly work on your behalf.

POINTER Numbers doesn't always record things in chronological order. It is structured around descriptions of the two generations of Israelites rather than around a strict chronological sequence. For example, the things described by chapters 7-9 probably all took place before the census in chapter 1 (compare the dates in 9:1[17] and 1:1[18]).

READING 25 — NUMBERS 9:1-14

PLOT SUMMARY 9:1-14 provides instructions for the celebration of the Passover. 9:15-23 describes how God provided a cloud to guide the Israelites in their travels. 10:1-10 provides instructions for various uses of trumpets to communicate with the whole camp. 10:11-36 describes the beginning of Israel's travels from Mount Sinai into the wilderness.

And the Lord spoke to Moses in the wilderness of Sinai, in the first month of the second year after they had come out of the land of Egypt, saying, ² "Let the people of Israel keep the Passover at its appointed time. ³ On the fourteenth day of this month, at twilight, you shall keep it at its appointed time; according to all its statutes and all its rules you shall keep it." ⁴ So Moses told the people of Israel that they should keep the Passover. ⁵ And they kept the Passover in the first month, on the fourteenth day of the month, at twilight, in the wilderness of Sinai; according to all that the Lord commanded Moses, so the people of Israel did. ⁶ And there were certain men who were unclean through touching a dead body, so that they could not keep the Passover on that day, and they came before Moses and Aaron on that day. ⁷ And those men said to him, "We are unclean through touching a dead body. Why are we kept from bringing the Lord's offering at its appointed time among the people of Israel?" ⁸ And Moses said to them, "Wait, that I may hear what the Lord will command concerning you."

⁹ The Lord spoke to Moses, saying, ¹⁰ "Speak to the people of Israel, saying, If any one of you or of your descendants is unclean through touching a dead body, or is on a long journey, he shall still keep the Passover to the Lord. ¹¹ In the second month on the fourteenth day at twilight they shall keep it. They shall eat it with unleavened bread and bitter herbs. ¹² They shall leave none of it until the morning, nor break any of its bones; according to all the statute for the Passover they shall keep it. ¹³ But if anyone who is clean and is not on a journey fails to keep the Passover, that person shall be cut off from his people because he did not bring the Lord's offering at its appointed time; that man shall bear his sin. ¹⁴ And if a stranger sojourns among you and would keep the Passover to the Lord, according to the statute of the Passover and according to its rule, so shall he do. You shall have one statute, both for the sojourner and for the native."

1. What was the Passover festival designed to remind the Israelites of? (See Exodus 12 in the appendix for a reminder if you need one.)

---

17. And the Lord spoke to Moses in the wilderness of Sinai, in the first month of the second year after they had come out of the land of Egypt, saying ...
18. The Lord spoke to Moses in the wilderness of Sinai, in the tent of meeting, on the first day of the second month, in the second year after they had come out of the land of Egypt, saying ...

2. Why do you think it was important that even the unclean, travellers and strangers were free to celebrate it?

PONDER Read 1 Corinthians 5:6-8.[19] In what sense is Christ "our Passover lamb"?

PRAYER IDEAS Praise God for the provision of Christ, your Passover lamb. Ask him to strengthen you to "celebrate the festival" by living truthfully, in sincere obedience to Jesus (1 Cor 5:8).

READING 26 — NUMBERS 11:4-34

PLOT SUMMARY In chapter 11, the people of Israel begin to grumble against God because they are unsatisfied with what God has done and what he has provided for them.

Now the rabble that was among them had a strong craving. And the people of Israel also wept again and said, "Oh that we had meat to eat! [5] We remember the fish we ate in Egypt that cost nothing, the cucumbers, the melons, the leeks, the onions, and the garlic. [6] But now our strength is dried up, and there is nothing at all but this manna to look at."

[7] Now the manna was like coriander seed, and its appearance like that of bdellium. [8] The people went about and gathered it and ground it in handmills or beat it in mortars and boiled it in pots and made cakes of it. And the taste of it was like the taste of cakes baked with oil. [9] When the dew fell upon the camp in the night, the manna fell with it.

[10] Moses heard the people weeping throughout their clans, everyone at the door of his tent. And the anger of the LORD blazed hotly, and Moses was displeased. [11] Moses said to the LORD, "Why have you dealt ill with your servant? And why have I not found favor in your sight, that you lay the burden of all this people on me? [12] Did I conceive all this people? Did I give them birth, that you should say to me, 'Carry them in your bosom, as a nurse carries a nursing child,' to the land that you swore to give their fathers? [13] Where am I to get meat to give to all this people? For they weep before me and say, 'Give us meat, that we may eat.' [14] I am not able to carry all this people alone; the burden is too heavy for me. [15] If you will treat me like this, kill me at once, if I find favor in your sight, that I may not see my wretchedness."

[16] Then the LORD said to Moses, "Gather for me seventy men of the elders of Israel, whom you know to be the elders of the people and officers over them, and bring them to the tent of meeting, and let them take their stand there with you. [17] And I will come down and talk with you there. And I will take some of the Spirit that is on you and put it on them, and they shall bear the burden of the people with you, so that you may not bear it yourself alone. [18] And say to the people, 'Consecrate yourselves for tomorrow, and you shall eat meat, for you have wept in the hearing of the LORD, saying, "Who will give us meat to eat? For it was better for us in Egypt." Therefore the LORD will give you meat, and you shall eat. [19] You shall not eat just one day, or two days, or five days, or ten days, or twenty days, [20] but a whole month, until it comes out at your nostrils and becomes loathsome to you,

---

19. Your boasting is not good. Do you not know that a little leaven leavens the whole lump? [7] Cleanse out the old leaven that you may be a new lump, as you really are unleavened. For Christ, our Passover lamb, has been sacrificed. [8] Let us therefore celebrate the festival, not with the old leaven, the leaven of malice and evil, but with the unleavened bread of sincerity and truth.

because you have rejected the Lord who is among you and have wept before him, saying, "Why did we come out of Egypt?"'" 21 But Moses said, "The people among whom I am number six hundred thousand on foot, and you have said, 'I will give them meat, that they may eat a whole month!' 22 Shall flocks and herds be slaughtered for them, and be enough for them? Or shall all the fish of the sea be gathered together for them, and be enough for them?" 23 And the Lord said to Moses, "Is the Lord's hand shortened? Now you shall see whether my word will come true for you or not."

24 So Moses went out and told the people the words of the Lord. And he gathered seventy men of the elders of the people and placed them around the tent. 25 Then the Lord came down in the cloud and spoke to him, and took some of the Spirit that was on him and put it on the seventy elders. And as soon as the Spirit rested on them, they prophesied. But they did not continue doing it.

26 Now two men remained in the camp, one named Eldad, and the other named Medad, and the Spirit rested on them. They were among those registered, but they had not gone out to the tent, and so they prophesied in the camp. 27 And a young man ran and told Moses, "Eldad and Medad are prophesying in the camp." 28 And Joshua the son of Nun, the assistant of Moses from his youth, said, "My lord Moses, stop them." 29 But Moses said to him, "Are you jealous for my sake? Would that all the Lord's people were prophets, that the Lord would put his Spirit on them!" 30 And Moses and the elders of Israel returned to the camp.

31 Then a wind from the Lord sprang up, and it brought quail from the sea and let them fall beside the camp, about a day's journey on this side and a day's journey on the other side, around the camp, and about two cubits above the ground. 32 And the people rose all that day and all night and all the next day, and gathered the quail. Those who gathered least gathered ten homers. And they spread them out for themselves all around the camp. 33 While the meat was yet between their teeth, before it was consumed, the anger of the Lord was kindled against the people, and the Lord struck down the people with a very great plague. 34 Therefore the name of that place was called Kibroth-hattaavah, because there they buried the people who had the craving.

1. Why were the people complaining?

2. How did Moses react?

3. How did God react?

PONDER Israel responded to a time of testing in the wilderness with hard-hearted rebellion. As a result, God was angry and punished them. How do you respond when your faith is tested?

PRAYER IDEAS Read Hebrews 3:7-12[20] and notice the way the author uses the example of the Israelites to warn you against evil and

---

20. Therefore, as the Holy Spirit says,

"Today, if you hear his voice,
8 do not harden your hearts as in the rebellion,
   on the day of testing in the wilderness,
9 where your fathers put me to the test
   and saw my works for forty years.
10 Therefore I was provoked with that generation,
   and said, 'They always go astray in their heart;
   they have not known my ways.'
11 As I swore in my wrath,
   'They shall not enter my rest.'"

12 Take care, brothers, lest there be in any of you an evil, unbelieving heart, leading you to fall away from the living God.

unbelief. Ask God to help you never to fall away from him.

POINTER Numbers 11 begins a new section in Numbers. In chapters 1-10, the author provides us with a picture of Israel as they ought to be. It's a picture full of potential—even idealism. But Numbers 11-25 shows us Israel as they really were (or, at least, what the generation that left Egypt was like).

READING 27 — NUMBERS 12:1-16

PLOT SUMMARY *Chapter 12 continues the 'grumbling' theme, but this time it's Moses' own brother and sister who are grumbling against him!*

Miriam and Aaron spoke against Moses because of the Cushite woman whom he had married, for he had married a Cushite woman. ² And they said, "Has the Lord indeed spoken only through Moses? Has he not spoken through us also?" And the Lord heard it. ³ Now the man Moses was very meek, more than all people who were on the face of the earth. ⁴ And suddenly the Lord said to Moses and to Aaron and Miriam, "Come out, you three, to the tent of meeting." And the three of them came out. ⁵ And the Lord came down in a pillar of cloud and stood at the entrance of the tent and called Aaron and Miriam, and they both came forward. ⁶ And he said, "Hear my words: If there is a prophet among you, I the Lord make myself known to him in a vision; I speak with him in a dream. ⁷ Not so with my servant Moses. He is faithful in all my house. ⁸ With him I speak mouth to mouth, clearly, and not in riddles, and he beholds the form of the Lord. Why then were you not afraid to speak against my servant Moses?" ⁹ And the anger of the Lord was kindled against them, and he departed.

¹⁰ When the cloud removed from over the tent, behold, Miriam was leprous, like snow. And Aaron turned toward Miriam, and behold, she was leprous. ¹¹ And Aaron said to Moses, "Oh, my lord, do not punish us because we have done foolishly and have sinned. ¹² Let her not be as one dead, whose flesh is half eaten away when he comes out of his mother's womb." ¹³ And Moses cried to the Lord, "O God, please heal her—please." ¹⁴ But the Lord said to Moses, "If her father had but spit in her face, should she not be shamed seven days? Let her be shut outside the camp seven days, and after that she may be brought in again." ¹⁵ So Miriam was shut outside the camp seven days, and the people did not set out on the march till Miriam was brought in again. ¹⁶ After that the people set out from Hazeroth, and camped in the wilderness of Paran.

1. What do you learn about Moses from this passage?

2. What do you think was the real issue behind Aaron and Miriam's complaints?

3. How did God respond to Aaron and Miriam?

4. What part did Moses play in the mercy God showed to Miriam after her punishment?

PONDER Why was disrespect towards Moses' leadership ultimately disrespect towards God?

PRAYER IDEAS Read Hebrews 3:1-3.[21] Praise God for Jesus, who is even greater than Moses. Ask God to help you to respect and submit to Jesus' leadership as you should.

READING 28 — NUMBERS 14:1-25

PLOT SUMMARY *Chapter 13 describes the exploration of the land of Canaan by a select group. They report that the land is good, but the people there are big and strong. All but one of them—Caleb—discourage the Israelites from trying to take possession of it. Chapter 14 describes the Israelite grumbling that followed.*

Then all the congregation raised a loud cry, and the people wept that night. [2] And all the people of Israel grumbled against Moses and Aaron. The whole congregation said to them, "Would that we had died in the land of Egypt! Or would that we had died in this wilderness! [3] Why is the LORD bringing us into this land, to fall by the sword? Our wives and our little ones will become a prey. Would it not be better for us to go back to Egypt?" [4] And they said to one another, "Let us choose a leader and go back to Egypt."

[5] Then Moses and Aaron fell on their faces before all the assembly of the congregation of the people of Israel. [6] And Joshua the son of Nun and Caleb the son of Jephunneh, who were among those who had spied out the land, tore their clothes [7] and said to all the congregation of the people of Israel, "The land, which we passed through to spy it out, is an exceedingly good land. [8] If the LORD delights in us, he will bring us into this land and give it to us, a land that flows with milk and honey. [9] Only do not rebel against the LORD. And do not fear the people of the land, for they are bread for us. Their protection is removed from them, and the LORD is with us; do not fear them." [10] Then all the congregation said to stone them with stones. But the glory of the LORD appeared at the tent of meeting to all the people of Israel.

[11] And the LORD said to Moses, "How long will this people despise me? And how long will they not believe in me, in spite of all the signs that I have done among them? [12] I will strike them with the pestilence and disinherit them, and I will make of you a nation greater and mightier than they."

[13] But Moses said to the LORD, "Then the Egyptians will hear of it, for you brought up this people in your might from among them, [14] and they will tell the inhabitants of this land. They have heard that you, O LORD, are in the midst of this people. For you, O LORD, are seen face to face, and your cloud stands over them and you go before them, in a pillar of cloud by day and in a pillar of fire by night. [15] Now if you kill this people as one man, then the nations who have heard your fame will say, [16] 'It is because the LORD was not able to bring this people into the land that he swore to give to them that he has killed them in the wilderness.' [17] And now, please let the power of the Lord be great as you have promised, saying, [18] 'The LORD is slow to anger and abounding in steadfast love, forgiving iniquity and transgression, but he will by no means clear the guilty, visiting the iniquity of the fathers on the children, to the third

---

[21]. Therefore, holy brothers, you who share in a heavenly calling, consider Jesus, the apostle and high priest of our confession, [2] who was faithful to him who appointed him, just as Moses also was faithful in all God's house. [3] For Jesus has been counted worthy of more glory than Moses—as much more glory as the builder of a house has more honor than the house itself.

and the fourth generation.' ¹⁹ Please pardon the iniquity of this people, according to the greatness of your steadfast love, just as you have forgiven this people, from Egypt until now."

²⁰ Then the LORD said, "I have pardoned, according to your word. ²¹ But truly, as I live, and as all the earth shall be filled with the glory of the LORD, ²² none of the men who have seen my glory and my signs that I did in Egypt and in the wilderness, and yet have put me to the test these ten times and have not obeyed my voice, ²³ shall see the land that I swore to give to their fathers. And none of those who despised me shall see it. ²⁴ But my servant Caleb, because he has a different spirit and has followed me fully, I will bring into the land into which he went, and his descendants shall possess it. ²⁵ Now, since the Amalekites and the Canaanites dwell in the valleys, turn tomorrow and set out for the wilderness by the way to the Red Sea."

1. Joshua and Caleb pleaded with the people not to fear (vv. 5-9). What reasons did they give for why the people should trust God?

2. Moses pleaded with God to forgive his people (vv. 13-19). What reasons did he give for why God should?

3. What tragic judgement did God pronounce upon this generation (vv. 22-23)?

PONDER Read 1 Corinthians 10:1-13 in the appendix (pp. 74-75). What lessons do you to learn from this generation?

PRAYER IDEAS Praise God for being as gracious as he's described in verse 18. Ask him to strengthen you so you will learn the lessons of this generation of Israelites.

READING 29   NUMBERS 16:1-35

PLOT SUMMARY *Chapter 15 presents instructions for various sacrificial offerings, and then describes the punishment of a Sabbath-breaker, as well as God's instructions about tassels on garments, which serve to remind the Israelites of the need to obey.*

Now Korah the son of Izhar, son of Kohath, son of Levi, and Dathan and Abiram the sons of Eliab, and On the son of Peleth, sons of Reuben, took men. ² And they rose up before Moses, with a number of the people of Israel, 250 chiefs of the congregation, chosen from the assembly, well-known men. ³ They assembled themselves together against Moses and against Aaron and said to them, "You have gone too far! For all in the congregation are holy, every one of them, and the LORD is among them. Why then do you exalt yourselves above the assembly of the LORD?" ⁴ When Moses heard it, he fell on his face, ⁵ and he said to Korah and all his company, "In the morning the LORD will show who is his, and who is holy, and will bring him near to him. The one whom he chooses he will bring near to him. ⁶ Do this: take censers, Korah and all his company; ⁷ put fire in them and put incense on them before the LORD tomorrow, and the man whom the LORD chooses shall be the holy one. You have gone too far, sons of Levi!" ⁸ And Moses said to Korah, "Hear now, you sons of Levi: ⁹ is it too small a thing for you that the God of Israel has separated you from the congregation of Israel, to bring you near to himself, to do service in the tabernacle of the Lord and to stand before the congregation to minister to them, [10] and that he has brought you near him, and all your brothers the sons of Levi with you? And would you seek the priesthood also? [11] Therefore it is against the Lord that you and all your company have gathered together. What is Aaron that you grumble against him?"

[12] And Moses sent to call Dathan and Abiram the sons of Eliab, and they said, "We will not come up. [13] Is it a small thing that you have brought us up out of a land flowing with milk and honey, to kill us in the wilderness, that you must also make yourself a prince over us? [14] Moreover, you have not brought us into a land flowing with milk and honey, nor given us inheritance of fields and vineyards. Will you put out the eyes of these men? We will not come up." [15] And Moses was very angry and said to the Lord, "Do not respect their offering. I have not taken one donkey from them, and I have not harmed one of them."

[16] And Moses said to Korah, "Be present, you and all your company, before the Lord, you and they, and Aaron, tomorrow. [17] And let every one of you take his censer and put incense on it, and every one of you bring before the Lord his censer, 250 censers; you also, and Aaron, each his censer." [18] So every man took his censer and put fire in them and laid incense on them and stood at the entrance of the tent of meeting with Moses and Aaron. [19] Then Korah assembled all the congregation against them at the entrance of the tent of meeting. And the glory of the Lord appeared to all the congregation.

[20] And the Lord spoke to Moses and to Aaron, saying, [21] "Separate yourselves from among this congregation, that I may consume them in a moment." [22] And they fell on their faces and said, "O God, the God of the spirits of all flesh, shall one man sin, and will you be angry with all the congregation?" [23] And the Lord spoke to Moses, saying, [24] "Say to the congregation, Get away from the dwelling of Korah, Dathan, and Abiram."

[25] Then Moses rose and went to Dathan and Abiram, and the elders of Israel followed him. [26] And he spoke to the congregation, saying, "Depart, please, from the tents of these wicked men, and touch nothing of theirs, lest you be swept away with all their sins." [27] So they got away from the dwelling of Korah, Dathan, and Abiram. And Dathan and Abiram came out and stood at the door of their tents, together with their wives, their sons, and their little ones. [28] And Moses said, "Hereby you shall know that the Lord has sent me to do all these works, and that it has not been of my own accord. [29] If these men die as all men die, or if they are visited by the fate of all mankind, then the Lord has not sent me. [30] But if the Lord creates something new, and the ground opens its mouth and swallows them up with all that belongs to them, and they go down alive into Sheol, then you shall know that these men have despised the Lord."

[31] And as soon as he had finished speaking all these words, the ground under them split apart. [32] And the earth opened its mouth and swallowed them up, with their households and all the people who belonged to Korah and all their goods. [33] So they and all that belonged to them went down alive into Sheol, and the earth closed over them, and they perished from the midst of the assembly. [34] And all Israel who were around them fled at their cry, for they said, "Lest the earth swallow us up!" [35] And fire came out from the Lord and consumed the 250 men offering the incense.

1. What were Korah and the others upset about?

2. Why did Moses say they have "despised the LORD" (v. 30)?

PONDER Read Jude 3-4 and 11.[22] What sort of pattern does Korah's rebellion lay down for those who oppose God in future generations? Do you conform to this pattern?

PRAYER IDEAS Ask God to help you to "contend for the faith" in the face of false teaching (Jude 3), stand up for the truth and live in obedience to Jesus.

READING 30 — NUMBERS 19:1-22

PLOT SUMMARY *In chapter 17, God reinforces Aaron's authority within Israel (by causing his staff to grow almonds!). In chapter 18, God outlines the responsibilities that Aaron and the other priests and Levites have within Israel, as well as the provision God has made for them. Chapter 19 contains instructions for cleansing the unclean.*

Now the LORD spoke to Moses and to Aaron, saying, 2 "This is the statute of the law that the LORD has commanded: Tell the people of Israel to bring you a red heifer without defect, in which there is no blemish, and on which a yoke has never come. 3 And you shall give it to Eleazar the priest, and it shall be taken outside the camp and slaughtered before him. 4 And Eleazar the priest shall take some of its blood with his finger, and sprinkle some of its blood toward the front of the tent of meeting seven times. 5 And the heifer shall be burned in his sight. Its skin, its flesh, and its blood, with its dung, shall be burned. 6 And the priest shall take cedarwood and hyssop and scarlet yarn, and throw them into the fire burning the heifer. 7 Then the priest shall wash his clothes and bathe his body in water, and afterward he may come into the camp. But the priest shall be unclean until evening.

8 The one who burns the heifer shall wash his clothes in water and bathe his body in water and shall be unclean until evening. 9 And a man who is clean shall gather up the ashes of the heifer and deposit them outside the camp in a clean place. And they shall be kept for the water for impurity for the congregation of the people of Israel; it is a sin offering. 10 And the one who gathers the ashes of the heifer shall wash his clothes and be unclean until evening. And this shall be a perpetual statute for the people of Israel, and for the stranger who sojourns among them.

11 "Whoever touches the dead body of any person shall be unclean seven days. 12 He shall cleanse himself with the water on the third day and on the seventh day, and so be clean. But if he does not cleanse himself on the third day and on the seventh day, he will not become clean. 13 Whoever touches a dead person, the body of anyone who has died, and does not cleanse himself, defiles the tabernacle of the LORD, and that person shall be cut off from Israel; because the water for impurity was not thrown on him, he shall be unclean. His uncleanness is still on him.

14 "This is the law when someone dies in a tent: everyone who comes into the tent and everyone who is in the tent shall be unclean

---

22. Beloved, although I was very eager to write to you about our common salvation, I found it necessary to write appealing to you to contend for the faith that was once for all delivered to the saints. 4 For certain people have crept in unnoticed who long ago were designated for this condemnation, ungodly people, who pervert the grace of our God into sensuality and deny our only Master and Lord, Jesus Christ ... 11 Woe to them! For they walked in the way of Cain and abandoned themselves for the sake of gain to Balaam's error and perished in Korah's rebellion."

seven days. ¹⁵ And every open vessel that has no cover fastened on it is unclean. ¹⁶ Whoever in the open field touches someone who was killed with a sword or who died naturally, or touches a human bone or a grave, shall be unclean seven days. ¹⁷ For the unclean they shall take some ashes of the burnt sin offering, and fresh water shall be added in a vessel. ¹⁸ Then a clean person shall take hyssop and dip it in the water and sprinkle it on the tent and on all the furnishings and on the persons who were there and on whoever touched the bone, or the slain or the dead or the grave. ¹⁹ And the clean person shall sprinkle it on the unclean on the third day and on the seventh day. Thus on the seventh day he shall cleanse him, and he shall wash his clothes and bathe himself in water, and at evening he shall be clean.

²⁰ "If the man who is unclean does not cleanse himself, that person shall be cut off from the midst of the assembly, since he has defiled the sanctuary of the LORD. Because the water for impurity has not been thrown on him, he is unclean. ²¹ And it shall be a statute forever for them. The one who sprinkles the water for impurity shall wash his clothes, and the one who touches the water for impurity shall be unclean until evening. ²² And whatever the unclean person touches shall be unclean, and anyone who touches it shall be unclean until evening."

1. What sorts of things made Israelites unclean?

2. What needed to be done to bring cleansing?

3. What does the need for a "sin offering" (v. 9) tell you about how seriously God regards uncleanness?

PONDER Read Hebrews 9:13-14.²³ How is Christ's blood better than "the blood of goats and bulls" and "the ashes of a heifer"?

PRAYER IDEAS Thank God for Jesus' generous sacrifice. Now that you've been purified, ask him to give you the strength to serve him.

READING 31 — NUMBERS 21:4-9

PLOT SUMMARY Chapter 20 records more Israelite grumbling, the incident that means even Moses will be prevented from entering the Promised Land, the deaths of Miriam and Aaron, and the way the Edomites hinder Israel's journey. Chapter 21 describes more of Israel's travels through the wilderness, some of the enemies they encounter on the way, and still more Israelite grumbling.

From Mount Hor they set out by the way to the Red Sea, to go around the land of Edom. And the people became impatient on the way. ⁵ And the people spoke against God and against Moses, "Why have you brought us up out of Egypt to die in the wilderness? For there is no food and no water, and we loathe this worthless food." ⁶ Then the LORD sent fiery serpents among the people, and they bit the

---

23. For if the blood of goats and bulls, and the sprinkling of defiled persons with the ashes of a heifer, sanctify for the purification of the flesh, ¹⁴ how much more will the blood of Christ, who through the eternal Spirit offered himself without blemish to God, purify our conscience from dead works to serve the living God.

people, so that many people of Israel died. ⁷ And the people came to Moses and said, "We have sinned, for we have spoken against the LORD and against you. Pray to the LORD, that he take away the serpents from us." So Moses prayed for the people. ⁸ And the LORD said to Moses, "Make a fiery serpent and set it on a pole, and everyone who is bitten, when he sees it, shall live." ⁹ So Moses made a bronze serpent and set it on a pole. And if a serpent bit anyone, he would look at the bronze serpent and live.

1. Why was God so angry with his people?

2. What was Moses' role in this incident?

3. What did the people need to do in order to live?

PONDER Read John 3:14-16.[24] How is Jesus similar to the bronze serpent? How is he different?

PRAYER IDEAS Praise God for his love for the world. Praise him for providing a way for rebels like you to be saved. Praise him for the remarkable offer of eternal life.

READING 32 — NUMBERS 22:1-35

PLOT SUMMARY *Chapters 22-24 tell the story of Balaam (a kind of prophet) and Balak (the King of Moab). The Moabites were fearful of the Israelites, so Balak sought to secure the services of Balaam to pronounce a curse upon Israel.*

Then the people of Israel set out and camped in the plains of Moab beyond the Jordan at Jericho. ² And Balak the son of Zippor saw all that Israel had done to the Amorites. ³ And Moab was in great dread of the people, because they were many. Moab was overcome with fear of the people of Israel. ⁴ And Moab said to the elders of Midian, "This horde will now lick up all that is around us, as the ox licks up the grass of the field." So Balak the son of Zippor, who was king of Moab at that time, ⁵ sent messengers to Balaam the son of Beor at Pethor, which is near the River in the land of the people of Amaw, to call him, saying, "Behold, a people has come out of Egypt. They cover the face of the earth, and they are dwelling opposite me. ⁶ Come now, curse this people for me, since they are too mighty for me. Perhaps I shall be able to defeat them and drive them from the land, for I know that he whom you bless is blessed, and he whom you curse is cursed."

⁷ So the elders of Moab and the elders of Midian departed with the fees for divination in their hand. And they came to Balaam and gave him Balak's message. ⁸ And he said to them, "Lodge here tonight, and I will bring back word to you, as the LORD speaks to me." So the princes of Moab stayed with Balaam. ⁹ And God came to Balaam and said, "Who are these men with you?" ¹⁰ And Balaam said to God, "Balak the son of Zippor, king of Moab, has sent to me, saying, ¹¹ 'Behold, a people

---

[24] "And as Moses lifted up the serpent in the wilderness, so must the Son of Man be lifted up, ¹⁵ that whoever believes in him may have eternal life."

¹⁶ "For God so loved the world, that he gave his only Son, that whoever believes in him should not perish but have eternal life."

has come out of Egypt, and it covers the face of the earth. Now come, curse them for me. Perhaps I shall be able to fight against them and drive them out.'" ¹² God said to Balaam, "You shall not go with them. You shall not curse the people, for they are blessed." ¹³ So Balaam rose in the morning and said to the princes of Balak, "Go to your own land, for the LORD has refused to let me go with you." ¹⁴ So the princes of Moab rose and went to Balak and said, "Balaam refuses to come with us."

¹⁵ Once again Balak sent princes, more in number and more honorable than these. ¹⁶ And they came to Balaam and said to him, "Thus says Balak the son of Zippor: 'Let nothing hinder you from coming to me, ¹⁷ for I will surely do you great honor, and whatever you say to me I will do. Come, curse this people for me.'" ¹⁸ But Balaam answered and said to the servants of Balak, "Though Balak were to give me his house full of silver and gold, I could not go beyond the command of the LORD my God to do less or more. ¹⁹ So you, too, please stay here tonight, that I may know what more the LORD will say to me." ²⁰ And God came to Balaam at night and said to him, "If the men have come to call you, rise, go with them; but only do what I tell you." ²¹ So Balaam rose in the morning and saddled his donkey and went with the princes of Moab.

²² But God's anger was kindled because he went, and the angel of the LORD took his stand in the way as his adversary. Now he was riding on the donkey, and his two servants were with him. ²³ And the donkey saw the angel of the LORD standing in the road, with a drawn sword in his hand. And the donkey turned aside out of the road and went into the field. And Balaam struck the donkey, to turn her into the road. ²⁴ Then the angel of the LORD stood in a narrow path between the vineyards, with a wall on either side. ²⁵ And when the donkey saw the angel of the LORD, she pushed against the wall and pressed Balaam's foot against the wall. So he struck her again. ²⁶ Then the angel of the LORD went ahead and stood in a narrow place, where there was no way to turn either to the right or to the left. ²⁷ When the donkey saw the angel of the LORD, she lay down under Balaam. And Balaam's anger was kindled, and he struck the donkey with his staff. ²⁸ Then the LORD opened the mouth of the donkey, and she said to Balaam, "What have I done to you, that you have struck me these three times?" ²⁹ And Balaam said to the donkey, "Because you have made a fool of me. I wish I had a sword in my hand, for then I would kill you." ³⁰ And the donkey said to Balaam, "Am I not your donkey, on which you have ridden all your life long to this day? Is it my habit to treat you this way?" And he said, "No."

³¹ Then the LORD opened the eyes of Balaam, and he saw the angel of the LORD standing in the way, with his drawn sword in his hand. And he bowed down and fell on his face. ³² And the angel of the LORD said to him, "Why have you struck your donkey these three times? Behold, I have come out to oppose you because your way is perverse before me. ³³ The donkey saw me and turned aside before me these three times. If she had not turned aside from me, surely just now I would have killed you and let her live." ³⁴ Then Balaam said to the angel of the LORD, "I have sinned, for I did not know that you stood in the road against me. Now therefore, if it is evil in your sight, I will turn back." ³⁵ And the angel of the LORD said to Balaam, "Go with the men, but speak only the word that I tell you." So Balaam went on with the princes of Balak.

1. Why were Balak and the Moabites fearful of Israel?

2. Why did God tell Balaam not to go to Balak (v. 12)?

3. Why do you think Balaam went to see Balak?

4. Why was God angry with Balaam?

PONDER Read 2 Peter 2:1,[25] 15-16.[26] What does Peter tell you about Balaam? What extra light does this shed on why God was angry with Balaam?

PRAYER IDEAS Ask God to work in you so that you will never be a person who ignores his word for the sake of financial gain. Also ask him to prevent you from ever heeding the teaching of someone like that.

READING 33 — NUMBERS 23:11-24

PLOT SUMMARY Chapters 23-24 record the oracles Balaam pronounced about Israel—not curses, as Balak had hoped, but instead words of blessing.

And Balak said to Balaam, "What have you done to me? I took you to curse my enemies, and behold, you have done nothing but bless them." [12] And he answered and said, "Must I not take care to speak what the LORD puts in my mouth?"

[13] And Balak said to him, "Please come with me to another place, from which you may see them. You shall see only a fraction of them and shall not see them all. Then curse them for me from there." [14] And he took him to the field of Zophim, to the top of Pisgah, and built seven altars and offered a bull and a ram on each altar. [15] Balaam said to Balak, "Stand here beside your burnt offering, while I meet the LORD over there." [16] And the LORD met Balaam and put a word in his mouth and said, "Return to Balak, and thus shall you speak." [17] And he came to him, and behold, he was standing beside his burnt offering, and the princes of Moab with him. And Balak said to him, "What has the LORD spoken?" [18] And Balaam took up his discourse and said,

"Rise, Balak, and hear;
  give ear to me, O son of Zippor:
[19] God is not man, that he should lie,
  or a son of man, that he should change his mind.
Has he said, and will he not do it?
  Or has he spoken, and will he not fulfill it?
[20] Behold, I received a command to bless:
  he has blessed, and I cannot revoke it.
[21] He has not beheld misfortune in Jacob,
  nor has he seen trouble in Israel.
The LORD their God is with them,
  and the shout of a king is among them.
[22] God brings them out of Egypt
  and is for them like the horns of the wild ox.
[23] For there is no enchantment against Jacob,
  no divination against Israel;
now it shall be said of Jacob and Israel,
  'What has God wrought!'
[24] Behold, a people! As a lioness it rises up

---

[25] But false prophets also arose among the people, just as there will be false teachers among you, who will secretly bring in destructive heresies, even denying the Master who bought them, bringing upon themselves swift destruction. [26] Forsaking the right way, they have gone astray. They have followed the way of Balaam, the son of Beor, who loved gain from wrongdoing, [16] but was rebuked for his own transgression; a speechless donkey spoke with human voice and restrained the prophet's madness.

and as a lion it lifts itself;
it does not lie down until it has devoured
the prey
and drunk the blood of the slain."

1. What sort of constraints did Balaam say he was under (vv. 12, 20)?

2. What did Balaam tell Balak about God?

3. What did Balaam tell Balak about Israel?

PONDER Read Genesis 12:1-3.[27] What did God promise Abraham and Abraham's descendents, the Israelites? Where in this passage do you see the continuation of these promises?

PRAYER IDEAS Read Galatians 3:25-29.[28] Thank God for counting even the Gentiles as Abraham's descendants in Christ. Thank him for deciding to bless you as one of Abraham's 'offspring'. Praise him for not changing his mind.

READING 34 — NUMBERS 25:1-18

PLOT SUMMARY Chapter 25 shows what happens when Israel intermingles with foreign nations.

While Israel lived in Shittim, the people began to whore with the daughters of Moab. 2 These invited the people to the sacrifices of their gods, and the people ate and bowed down to their gods. 3 So Israel yoked himself to Baal of Peor. And the anger of the LORD was kindled against Israel. 4 And the LORD said to Moses, "Take all the chiefs of the people and hang them in the sun before the LORD, that the fierce anger of the LORD may turn away from Israel." 5 And Moses said to the judges of Israel, "Each of you kill those of his men who have yoked themselves to Baal of Peor."

6 And behold, one of the people of Israel came and brought a Midianite woman to his family, in the sight of Moses and in the sight of the whole congregation of the people of Israel, while they were weeping in the entrance of the tent of meeting. 7 When Phinehas the son of Eleazar, son of Aaron the priest, saw it, he rose and left the congregation and took a spear in his hand 8 and went after the man of Israel into the chamber and pierced both of them, the man of Israel and the woman through her belly. Thus the plague on the people of Israel was stopped. 9 Nevertheless, those who died by the plague were twenty-four thousand.

10 And the LORD said to Moses, 11 "Phinehas the son of Eleazar, son of Aaron the priest, has turned back my wrath from the people of Israel, in that he was jealous with my jealousy among them, so that I did not consume the

---

[27]. Now the LORD said to Abram, "Go from your country and your kindred and your father's house to the land that I will show you. 2 And I will make of you a great nation, and I will bless you and make your name great, so that you will be a blessing. 3 I will bless those who bless you, and him who dishonors you I will curse, and in you all the families of the earth shall be blessed."

[28]. But now that faith has come, we are no longer under a guardian, 26 for in Christ Jesus you are all sons of God, through faith. 27 For as many of you as were baptized into Christ have put on Christ. 28 There is neither Jew nor Greek, there is neither slave nor free, there is no male and female, for you are all one in Christ Jesus. 29 And if you are Christ's, then you are Abraham's offspring, heirs according to promise.

people of Israel in my jealousy. ¹² Therefore say, 'Behold, I give to him my covenant of peace, ¹³ and it shall be to him and to his descendants after him the covenant of a perpetual priesthood, because he was jealous for his God and made atonement for the people of Israel.'"

¹⁴ The name of the slain man of Israel, who was killed with the Midianite woman, was Zimri the son of Salu, chief of a father's house belonging to the Simeonites. ¹⁵ And the name of the Midianite woman who was killed was Cozbi the daughter of Zur, who was the tribal head of a father's house in Midian.

¹⁶ And the LORD spoke to Moses, saying, ¹⁷ "Harass the Midianites and strike them down, ¹⁸ for they have harassed you with their wiles, with which they beguiled you in the matter of Peor, and in the matter of Cozbi, the daughter of the chief of Midian, their sister, who was killed on the day of the plague on account of Peor."

1. What did Israel do to 'kindle' the anger of the Lord against them?

2. How did Phinehas 'turn back' God's anger from the Israelites?

3. Why was God so pleased with Phinehas?

PONDER Read Romans 12:11.²⁹ How is Phinehas a great model of a life lived in zealous (or jealous) service of God?

PRAYER IDEAS Ask God to change your heart so that you will care for his honour as much as he does. Confess your half-heartedness. Ask him to help you to be zealous and fervent in your service of Christ.

POINTER We may presume that jealousy is an ungodly trait in a person, but the Bible is clear that God himself is jealous because he loves his people so intensely (e.g. Exod 34:13-14³⁰).

READING 35 — NUMBERS 27:12-23

PLOT SUMMARY *Chapter 26 is the second major census or 'numbering' in the book. It is the numbering of the second generation—those who will enter the land God promised. The chapter ends with instructions on how the land should be divided between them. Chapter 27 begins with a test case about the provision of land, and then concludes with the handover of leadership from Moses to Joshua.*

The LORD said to Moses, "Go up into this mountain of Abarim and see the land that I have given to the people of Israel. ¹³ When you have seen it, you also shall be gathered to your people, as your brother Aaron was, ¹⁴ because you rebelled against my word in the wilderness of Zin when the congregation quarreled, failing to uphold me as holy at the waters before their eyes." (These are the waters of Meribah of Kadesh in the wilderness

---

29. Do not be slothful in zeal, be fervent in spirit, serve the Lord.
30. You shall tear down their altars and break their pillars and cut down their Asherim ¹⁴ (for you shall worship no other god, for the LORD, whose name is Jealous, is a jealous God) ...

of Zin.) [15] Moses spoke to the LORD, saying, [16] "Let the LORD, the God of the spirits of all flesh, appoint a man over the congregation [17] who shall go out before them and come in before them, who shall lead them out and bring them in, that the congregation of the LORD may not be as sheep that have no shepherd." [18] So the LORD said to Moses, "Take Joshua the son of Nun, a man in whom is the Spirit, and lay your hand on him. [19] Make him stand before Eleazar the priest and all the congregation, and you shall commission him in their sight. [20] You shall invest him with some of your authority, that all the congregation of the people of Israel may obey. [21] And he shall stand before Eleazar the priest, who shall inquire for him by the judgment of the Urim before the LORD. At his word they shall go out, and at his word they shall come in, both he and all the people of Israel with him, the whole congregation." [22] And Moses did as the LORD commanded him. He took Joshua and made him stand before Eleazar the priest and the whole congregation, [23] and he laid his hands on him and commissioned him as the LORD directed through Moses.

1. Why was Moses prohibited from entering the land? (See also 20:2-13 in the appendix, p. 75.)

2. What did God say Joshua's role will be like in Israel?

3. What evidence in Numbers have you seen that Israel were sheep who needed a shepherd (cf. Matt 9:36[31])?

PONDER How did God continue to provide for his people in this passage? What does this tell you about God's generosity?

PRAYER IDEAS Thank God for never leaving his people leaderless. Thank God especially for your leader—Jesus, the good shepherd. Praise him for his compassion.

POINTER Numbers 26:1 begins the third and final section in the book of Numbers. The handover from Moses to Joshua marks the very end of the first generation of Israelites. Chapters 26-36 describe the new generation—those who will actually enter the Promised Land. Notice the significant verses: 26:63-65.[32]

READING 36 — NUMBERS 28:1-8

PLOT SUMMARY Chapters 28-29 contain instructions for various offerings that the Israelites were to bring to God at different times.

The LORD spoke to Moses, saying, [2] "Command the people of Israel and say to them, 'My offering, my food for my food offerings, my pleasing aroma, you shall be careful to offer

---

[31]. When he saw the crowds, he had compassion for them, because they were harassed and helpless, like sheep without a shepherd.
[32]. These were those listed by Moses and Eleazar the priest, who listed the people of Israel in the plains of Moab by the Jordan at Jericho. [64] But among these there was not one of those listed by Moses and Aaron the priest, who had listed the people of Israel in the wilderness of Sinai. [65] For the LORD had said of them, "They shall die in the wilderness." Not one of them was left, except Caleb the son of Jephunneh and Joshua the son of Nun.

to me at its appointed time.' ³ And you shall say to them, This is the food offering that you shall offer to the LORD: two male lambs a year old without blemish, day by day, as a regular offering. ⁴ The one lamb you shall offer in the morning, and the other lamb you shall offer at twilight; ⁵ also a tenth of an ephah of fine flour for a grain offering, mixed with a quarter of a hin of beaten oil. ⁶ It is a regular burnt offering, which was ordained at Mount Sinai for a pleasing aroma, a food offering to the LORD. ⁷ Its drink offering shall be a quarter of a hin for each lamb. In the Holy Place you shall pour out a drink offering of strong drink to the LORD. ⁸ The other lamb you shall offer at twilight. Like the grain offering of the morning, and like its drink offering, you shall offer it as a food offering, with a pleasing aroma to the LORD."

1. Why do you think the lambs offered had to be "without blemish" (v. 3)?

2. What instructions did God give about the daily offering?

3. How does God feel about the offering when it is done properly (vv. 2, 6, 8)?

PONDER Read 1 Peter 1:17-19.³³ What does this passage tell you about Christ and what he has done for you? What does Numbers 28:1-8 add to your understanding of this?

PRAYER IDEAS Praise God for what Christ's perfect sacrifice achieved—obedience in place of our disobedience, and rescue from a futile way of life.

READING 37 — NUMBERS 30:1-16

PLOT SUMMARY Chapter 30 contains instructions about keeping vows. Chapter 31 describes Israel's war against Midian (in retribution for their earlier harassment of the Israelites; see chapter 25, especially verses 16-18).

Moses spoke to the heads of the tribes of the people of Israel, saying, "This is what the LORD has commanded. ² If a man vows a vow to the LORD, or swears an oath to bind himself by a pledge, he shall not break his word. He shall do according to all that proceeds out of his mouth.
³ "If a woman vows a vow to the LORD and binds herself by a pledge, while within her father's house in her youth, ⁴ and her father hears of her vow and of her pledge by which she has bound herself and says nothing to her, then all her vows shall stand, and every pledge by which she has bound herself shall stand. ⁵ But if her father opposes her on the day that he hears of it, no vow of hers, no pledge by which she has bound herself shall

---

33. And if you call on him as Father who judges impartially according to each one's deeds, conduct yourselves with fear throughout the time of your exile, ¹⁸ knowing that you were ransomed from the futile ways inherited from your forefathers, not with perishable things such as silver or gold, ¹⁹ but with the precious blood of Christ, like that of a lamb without blemish or spot.

stand. And the Lord will forgive her, because her father opposed her.

6 "If she marries a husband, while under her vows or any thoughtless utterance of her lips by which she has bound herself, 7 and her husband hears of it and says nothing to her on the day that he hears, then her vows shall stand, and her pledges by which she has bound herself shall stand. 8 But if, on the day that her husband comes to hear of it, he opposes her, then he makes void her vow that was on her, and the thoughtless utterance of her lips by which she bound herself. And the Lord will forgive her. 9 (But any vow of a widow or of a divorced woman, anything by which she has bound herself, shall stand against her.) 10 And if she vowed in her husband's house or bound herself by a pledge with an oath, 11 and her husband heard of it and said nothing to her and did not oppose her, then all her vows shall stand, and every pledge by which she bound herself shall stand. 12 But if her husband makes them null and void on the day that he hears them, then whatever proceeds out of her lips concerning her vows or concerning her pledge of herself shall not stand. Her husband has made them void, and the Lord will forgive her. 13 Any vow and any binding oath to afflict herself, her husband may establish, or her husband may make void. 14 But if her husband says nothing to her from day to day, then he establishes all her vows or all her pledges that are upon her. He has established them, because he said nothing to her on the day that he heard of them. 15 But if he makes them null and void after he has heard of them, then he shall bear her iniquity."

16 These are the statutes that the Lord commanded Moses about a man and his wife and about a father and his daughter while she is in her youth within her father's house.

1. What does verse 2 tell you about vow-keeping?

2. Under what circumstances could a wife or daughter be released from a vow?

PONDER What does Numbers 23:19[34] tell you about God's attitude to his word? Read Matthew 5:33-37.[35] Given this reading's passage, what are the implications for you?

PRAYER IDEAS Praise God for his faithfulness to his word. Confess the ways in which you're not true to your word. Ask him to help you to be like him so that your 'yes' will be 'yes' and your 'no' will be 'no'.

READING 38 — NUMBERS 33:50-56

PLOT SUMMARY Chapter 32 describes the negotiations between Moses and the tribes of Reuben and Gad (and the half-tribe of Manasseh) over the land they would inherit, and how they would help the rest of the Israelites capture the land on the other side

---

34. God is not man, that he should lie,
    or a son of man, that he should change his mind.
    Has he said, and will he not do it?
    Or has he spoken, and will he not fulfill it?
35. "Again you have heard that it was said to those of old, 'You shall not swear falsely, but shall perform to the Lord what you have sworn.' 34 But I say to you, Do not take an oath at all, either by heaven, for it is the throne of God, 35 or by the earth, for it is his footstool, or by Jerusalem, for it is the city of the great King. 36 And do not take an oath by your head, for you cannot make one hair white or black. 37 Let what you say be simply 'Yes' or 'No'; anything more than this comes from evil."

of the Jordan river. Chapter 33 summarizes the journey Israel took from Egypt to the edge of the Promised Land, and then records God's instructions to them about entering the land.

And the LORD spoke to Moses in the plains of Moab by the Jordan at Jericho, saying, [51] "Speak to the people of Israel and say to them, When you pass over the Jordan into the land of Canaan, [52] then you shall drive out all the inhabitants of the land from before you and destroy all their figured stones and destroy all their metal images and demolish all their high places. [53] And you shall take possession of the land and settle in it, for I have given the land to you to possess it. [54] You shall inherit the land by lot according to your clans. To a large tribe you shall give a large inheritance, and to a small tribe you shall give a small inheritance. Wherever the lot falls for anyone, that shall be his. According to the tribes of your fathers you shall inherit. [55] But if you do not drive out the inhabitants of the land from before you, then those of them whom you let remain shall be as barbs in your eyes and thorns in your sides, and they shall trouble you in the land where you dwell. [56] And I will do to you as I thought to do to them."

1. What were the Israelites to do when they entered Canaan, the Promised Land?

2. What reasons did God give for doing these things?

PONDER Read 2 Corinthians 6:14-7:1.[36] Why are we not to be "unequally yoked with unbelievers"? What steps have you taken to "[bring] holiness to completion in the fear of God"?

PRAYER IDEAS Ask God to strengthen you to be loyal to him by separating yourself from the world around you. Praise him for his loyalty to you.

READING 39 — NUMBERS 27:1-11, 36:1-13

PLOT SUMMARY Chapter 34 describes the boundaries of the land Israel will inherit. Chapter 35 also contains laws for dealing with murder and accidental death.

Numbers 27:1-11

Then drew near the daughters of Zelophehad the son of Hepher, son of Gilead, son of Machir, son of Manasseh, from the clans of Manasseh the son of Joseph. The names of his daughters were: Mahlah, Noah, Hoglah, Milcah, and Tirzah. [2] And they stood before Moses and before Eleazar the priest and before the chiefs and all the congregation, at the entrance of the tent of meeting, saying, [3] "Our father died in the

---

[36]. Do not be unequally yoked with unbelievers. For what partnership has righteousness with lawlessness? Or what fellowship has light with darkness? [15] What accord has Christ with Belial? Or what portion does a believer share with an unbeliever? [16] What agreement has the temple of God with idols? For we are the temple of the living God; as God said,

"I will make my dwelling among them and walk among them,
and I will be their God,
and they shall be my people.

[17] Therefore go out from their midst,
and be separate from them, says the Lord,
and touch no unclean thing;
then I will welcome you,
[18] and I will be a father to you,
and you shall be sons and daughters to me,
says the Lord Almighty."

7:1 Since we have these promises, beloved, let us cleanse ourselves from every defilement of body and spirit, bringing holiness to completion in the fear of God.

wilderness. He was not among the company of those who gathered themselves together against the Lord in the company of Korah, but died for his own sin. And he had no sons. [4] Why should the name of our father be taken away from his clan because he had no son? Give to us a possession among our father's brothers."

[5] Moses brought their case before the Lord. [6] And the Lord said to Moses, [7] "The daughters of Zelophehad are right. You shall give them possession of an inheritance among their father's brothers and transfer the inheritance of their father to them. [8] And you shall speak to the people of Israel, saying, 'If a man dies and has no son, then you shall transfer his inheritance to his daughter. [9] And if he has no daughter, then you shall give his inheritance to his brothers. [10] And if he has no brothers, then you shall give his inheritance to his father's brothers. [11] And if his father has no brothers, then you shall give his inheritance to the nearest kinsman of his clan, and he shall possess it. And it shall be for the people of Israel a statute and rule, as the Lord commanded Moses.'"

Numbers 36:1-13

The heads of the fathers' houses of the clan of the people of Gilead the son of Machir, son of Manasseh, from the clans of the people of Joseph, came near and spoke before Moses and before the chiefs, the heads of the fathers' houses of the people of Israel. [2] They said, "The Lord commanded my lord to give the land for inheritance by lot to the people of Israel, and my lord was commanded by the Lord to give the inheritance of Zelophehad our brother to his daughters. [3] But if they are married to any of the sons of the other tribes of the people of Israel, then their inheritance will be taken from the inheritance of our fathers and added to the inheritance of the tribe into which they marry. So it will be taken away from the lot of our inheritance. [4] And when the jubilee of the people of Israel comes, then their inheritance will be added to the inheritance of the tribe into which they marry, and their inheritance will be taken from the inheritance of the tribe of our fathers."

[5] And Moses commanded the people of Israel according to the word of the Lord, saying, "The tribe of the people of Joseph is right. [6] This is what the Lord commands concerning the daughters of Zelophehad, 'Let them marry whom they think best, only they shall marry within the clan of the tribe of their father. [7] The inheritance of the people of Israel shall not be transferred from one tribe to another, for every one of the people of Israel shall hold on to the inheritance of the tribe of his fathers. [8] And every daughter who possesses an inheritance in any tribe of the people of Israel shall be wife to one of the clan of the tribe of her father, so that every one of the people of Israel may possess the inheritance of his fathers. [9] So no inheritance shall be transferred from one tribe to another, for each of the tribes of the people of Israel shall hold on to its own inheritance.'"

[10] The daughters of Zelophehad did as the Lord commanded Moses, [11] for Mahlah, Tirzah, Hoglah, Milcah, and Noah, the daughters of Zelophehad, were married to sons of their father's brothers. [12] They were married into the clans of the people of Manasseh the son of Joseph, and their inheritance remained in the tribe of their father's clan.

[13] These are the commandments and the rules that the Lord commanded through Moses to the people of Israel in the plains of Moab by the Jordan at Jericho.

1. In Numbers 27:1-11, why were Zelophehad's daughters concerned about losing their inheritance?

2. What was God's solution?

3. In Numbers 36:1-13, why were Zelophehad's relatives concerned about losing their inheritance?

4. What was God's solution?

PONDER God was faithful to his promises, ensuring that all Israel's tribes received their inheritance. Read 1 Peter 1:3-5.[37] What is the inheritance God has in store for you?

PRAYER IDEAS Praise God for his mercy and thank him for your imperishable inheritance in Christ.

POINTER The reference to the 'jubilee' in 36:4 refers back to Leviticus 25 (read it in the appendix, pp. 75-77—see especially verse 10). God decreed that every 50 years, all the land that had been lost to a family since the last jubilee would revert to being their property.

READING 40 — NUMBERS 32:1-13

Now the people of Reuben and the people of Gad had a very great number of livestock. And they saw the land of Jazer and the land of Gilead, and behold, the place was a place for livestock. [2] So the people of Gad and the people of Reuben came and said to Moses and to Eleazar the priest and to the chiefs of the congregation, [3] "Ataroth, Dibon, Jazer, Nimrah, Heshbon, Elealeh, Sebam, Nebo, and Beon, [4] the land that the LORD struck down before the congregation of Israel, is a land for livestock, and your servants have livestock." [5] And they said, "If we have found favor in your sight, let this land be given to your servants for a possession. Do not take us across the Jordan."

[6] But Moses said to the people of Gad and to the people of Reuben, "Shall your brothers go to the war while you sit here? [7] Why will you discourage the heart of the people of Israel from going over into the land that the LORD has given them? [8] Your fathers did this, when I sent them from Kadesh-barnea to see the land. [9] For when they went up to the Valley of Eshcol and saw the land, they discouraged the heart of the people of Israel from going into the land that the LORD had given them. [10] And the LORD's anger was kindled on that day, and he swore, saying, [11] 'Surely none of the men who came up out of Egypt, from twenty years old and upward, shall see the land that I swore to give to Abraham, to Isaac, and to Jacob, because they have not wholly followed me, [12] none except Caleb the son of Jephunneh the Kenizzite and Joshua the son of Nun, for they have wholly followed the LORD.' [13] And the LORD's anger was kindled against Israel, and he made them wander in the wilderness forty years, until all the generation that had done evil in the sight of the LORD was gone.

1. How well do verses 6-13 summarize the story of Numbers?

---

37. Blessed be the God and Father of our Lord Jesus Christ! According to his great mercy, he has caused us to be born again to a living hope through the resurrection of Jesus Christ from the dead, [4] to an inheritance that is imperishable, undefiled, and unfading, kept in heaven for you, [5] who by God's power are being guarded through faith for a salvation ready to be revealed in the last time.

2. What explanation do these verses give for Israel's wandering in the desert for so long?

3. What hint does verse 11 contain about why God persists with Israel?

PONDER What have you learned from the contrast Numbers presents between Israel's great unfaithfulness and God's patient and gracious faithfulness?

PRAYER IDEAS Thank God for all you've learned from the book of Numbers. Praise him for being faithful to his unfaithful people. Thank him for his faithfulness to you.

COLOSSIANS

INTRODUCTION

What makes you sit down and write a letter? Is it to catch up with someone? Is it to send all the gossip to relatives and friends? Or do you have a more serious message to convey?

Paul's New Testament letters are never just chatty social jottings. He certainly has little personal snippets in them, but, by and large, they have a serious, more weighty purpose. Colossians is no different.

Imagine a fertile valley with a delightful river wandering through it somewhere in what we now call Turkey. If you walked through the streets into the marketplace, you'd meet all kinds of people—Jews, Greeks who believe in mystery religions, and adherents to all sorts of other cults and philosophies. Among this smorgasbord of religions is a small group who call themselves 'Christians'. These were the people Paul was writing to in the letter we call Colossians.

We're not certain exactly when the Colossian church started. It may have been during Paul's lengthy stay in Ephesus (which was not far away). But whatever their past history, Paul is delighted with their faith in the gospel, and the fruit of that faith. However, he is concerned for their welfare—concerned enough to write to them while he is in prison.

You might like to use this prayer (or your own variation of it) before each of the next 20 studies:

Heavenly Father,
Please fill me with the knowledge of your will in all spiritual wisdom and understanding so that I can work in a manner worthy of you, fully pleasing to you, bearing fruit in every good work and increasing in the knowledge of you.
Amen.

READING 41 — COLOSSIANS 2:6-7

Therefore, as you received Christ Jesus the Lord, so walk in him, ⁷ rooted and built up in him and established in the faith, just as you were taught, abounding in thanksgiving.

Before tackling chapter 1, let's take a look at what are considered the summary verses of the whole letter. Consider memorizing them!

1. Paul says the Colossians had "received" Christ (v. 6). What does he mean (cf. Col 1:3-8,[38] 23[39])?

2. How were the Colossians to continue in their Christian 'walk' (v. 6)? How is this a response to the false teaching they faced?

3. In verse 7, the image is of the Colossians being like a tree whose roots are established or bedded down in Christ. How does this help you understand the way you are to continue in Christ?

PONDER Are you continuing in your walk with Christ? Are you growing?

PRAYER IDEAS Ask God to help you abound in thankfulness for your life in Christ.

POINTER Some think Paul wrote Colossians to combat a particular heresy in the Colossian church. However, there is little agreement about the details of this heresy (if there was one). In addition, the letter was meant for a wider readership than just the Colossian Christians (Col 4:16[40]). So you probably don't need to worry too much about what the 'heresy' actually was.

READING 42 — COLOSSIANS 2:6-7

Therefore, as you received Christ Jesus the Lord, so walk in him, [7] rooted and built up in him and established in the faith, just as you were taught, abounding in thanksgiving.

1. Paul says the Christian life is to be characterized by thankfulness, and lots of it (v. 7). How does this compare with:

a) your natural tendencies?

b) the national character of your country?

---

38. We always thank God, the Father of our Lord Jesus Christ, when we pray for you, [4] since we heard of your faith in Christ Jesus and of the love that you have for all the saints, [5] because of the hope laid up for you in heaven. Of this you have heard before in the word of the truth, the gospel, [6] which has come to you, as indeed in the whole world it is bearing fruit and growing—as it also does among you, since the day you heard it and understood the grace of God in truth, [7] just as you learned it from Epaphras our beloved fellow servant. He is a faithful minister of Christ on your behalf [8] and has made known to us your love in the Spirit.
39. ... if indeed you continue in the faith, stable and steadfast, not shifting from the hope of the gospel that you heard, which has been proclaimed in all creation under heaven, and of which I, Paul, became a minister.
40. And when this letter has been read among you, have it also read in the church of the Laodiceans; and see that you also read the letter from Laodicea.

2. From these verses, write down those words which indicate the past, completed actions and the present, continuing aspects of the Christian life.

Past	Present

3. From what you've learned in these two verses, what would you say to someone who is confused about what to do once they have begun the Christian life?

PONDER What things distract you from Jesus? What things tempt you to 'move on' from him?

PRAYER IDEAS Ask God to help you to continue to grow in your relationship with Jesus.

READING 43

COLOSSIANS 1:1-8

Paul, an apostle of Christ Jesus by the will of God, and Timothy our brother, ² To the saints and faithful brothers in Christ at Colossae:
Grace to you and peace from God our Father.
³ We always thank God, the Father of our Lord Jesus Christ, when we pray for you, ⁴ since we heard of your faith in Christ Jesus and of the love that you have for all the saints, ⁵ because of the hope laid up for you in heaven. Of this you have heard before in the word of the truth, the gospel, ⁶ which has come to you, as indeed in the whole world it is bearing fruit and growing—as it also does among you, since the day you heard it and understood the grace of God in truth, ⁷ just as you learned it from Epaphras our beloved fellow servant. He is a faithful minister of Christ on your behalf ⁸ and has made known to us your love in the Spirit.

Because Paul is so passionate about Christ and Christ alone being the answer to the false teaching the Colossians were struggling with, he tells us a great deal about Jesus and who he is. But he also speaks to the Colossian Christians in a very personal way.

1. What two things in the lives of the Colossians does Paul thank God for (v. 4)?

2. Where do these two things come from?

3. The Colossians "heard" the gospel, they "understood" it and they "learned" it from Epaphras (vv. 4, 6, 7). How does their experience influence the way Christians should engage in ministry?

PONDER In your own life, where do you see evidence of the "hope laid up for you in heaven" (v. 5)?

PRAYER IDEAS Thank God for all the things you learn about the gospel in verses 5-8.

READING 44 — COLOSSIANS 1:1-8

Paul, an apostle of Christ Jesus by the will of God, and Timothy our brother, ² To the saints and faithful brothers in Christ at Colossae:

Grace to you and peace from God our Father.

³ We always thank God, the Father of our Lord Jesus Christ, when we pray for you, ⁴ since we heard of your faith in Christ Jesus and of the love that you have for all the saints, ⁵ because of the hope laid up for you in heaven. Of this you have heard before in the word of the truth, the gospel, ⁶ which has come to you, as indeed in the whole world it is bearing fruit and growing—as it also does among you, since the day you heard it and understood the grace of God in truth, ⁷ just as you learned it from Epaphras our beloved fellow servant. He is a faithful minister of Christ on your behalf ⁸ and has made known to us your love in the Spirit.

1. What is "the hope laid up for you in heaven" (v. 5)?

2. Why is 'hope' a strange choice of words here? (Hint: think about how we use the word today.) What does this verse tell you about the nature of this hope?

3. Why is Paul so confident that the Colossians are Christians (vv. 6-8)?

PONDER How is the gospel "bearing fruit" in your life (v. 6)?

PRAYER IDEAS Thank God for "the hope laid up for you in heaven" (v. 5).

READING 45 — COLOSSIANS 1:1-14

Paul, an apostle of Christ Jesus by the will of God, and Timothy our brother, ² To the saints and faithful brothers in Christ at Colossae:

Grace to you and peace from God our Father.

³ We always thank God, the Father of our Lord Jesus Christ, when we pray for you, ⁴ since we heard of your faith in Christ Jesus and of the love that you have for all the saints, ⁵ because of the hope laid up for you in heaven. Of this you have heard before in

the word of the truth, the gospel, 6 which has come to you, as indeed in the whole world it is bearing fruit and growing—as it also does among you, since the day you heard it and understood the grace of God in truth, 7 just as you learned it from Epaphras our beloved fellow servant. He is a faithful minister of Christ on your behalf 8 and has made known to us your love in the Spirit.

9 And so, from the day we heard, we have not ceased to pray for you, asking that you may be filled with the knowledge of his will in all spiritual wisdom and understanding, 10 so as to walk in a manner worthy of the Lord, fully pleasing to him, bearing fruit in every good work and increasing in the knowledge of God. 11 May you be strengthened with all power, according to his glorious might, for all endurance and patience with joy, 12 giving thanks to the Father, who has qualified you to share in the inheritance of the saints in light. 13 He has delivered us from the domain of darkness and transferred us to the kingdom of his beloved Son, 14 in whom we have redemption, the forgiveness of sins.

1. Having affirmed their strengths, Paul tells the Colossians what he prays for them. What are Paul's main requests (vv. 9-11)?

2. What is the connection between the "knowledge of God" and the Colossians "bearing fruit" (vv. 9-10)?

3. How should you respond to what God has done for you in Christ?

PONDER What does this passage teach you about what to pray for others?

PRAYER IDEAS Pray for people in your church using some of the ideas in verses 9-14.

READING 46 — COLOSSIANS 1:15-20

He is the image of the invisible God, the firstborn of all creation. 16 For by him all things were created, in heaven and on earth, visible and invisible, whether thrones or dominions or rulers or authorities—all things were created through him and for him. 17 And he is before all things, and in him all things hold together. 18 And he is the head of the body, the church. He is the beginning, the firstborn from the dead, that in everything he might be preeminent. 19 For in him all the fullness of God was pleased to dwell, 20 and through him to reconcile to himself all things, whether on earth or in heaven, making peace by the blood of his cross.

1. What does it mean that Jesus is "the firstborn of all creation" and "the firstborn from the dead (vv. 15, 18)? (See also Psalm 89:27[41] and the pointers overleaf.)

2. How is Christ's supremacy demonstrated in verses 16-20?

---

41. And I will make him the firstborn,
    the highest of the kings of the earth.

all wisdom, that we may present everyone mature in Christ. 29 For this I toil, struggling with all his energy that he powerfully works within me.

2:1 For I want you to know how great a struggle I have for you and for those at Laodicea and for all who have not seen me face to face, 2 that their hearts may be encouraged, being knit together in love, to reach all the riches of full assurance of understanding and the knowledge of God's mystery, which is Christ, 3 in whom are hidden all the treasures of wisdom and knowledge. 4 I say this in order that no one may delude you with plausible arguments. 5 For though I am absent in body, yet I am with you in spirit, rejoicing to see your good order and the firmness of your faith in Christ.

1. What is Paul's goal (1:28-29)?

2. How does Paul achieve this goal?

3. The Gnostics (who propagated the type of heresy and false teaching that Paul was possibly addressing) believed that secret knowledge was the key to salvation. How does Paul's description of Christ defeat Gnostic arguments (2:3-4)?

PONDER How is 'warning' different to 'teaching' (1:28)?

PRAYER IDEAS Thank God for pastors/teachers who have ministries like Paul's—ministries that are focused on seeing people from all nations of the world grow to maturity in Christ.

READING 50 — COLOSSIANS 2:6-15

Therefore, as you received Christ Jesus the Lord, so walk in him, 7 rooted and built up in him and established in the faith, just as you were taught, abounding in thanksgiving.

8 See to it that no one takes you captive by philosophy and empty deceit, according to human tradition, according to the elemental spirits of the world, and not according to Christ. 9 For in him the whole fullness of deity dwells bodily, 10 and you have been filled in him, who is the head of all rule and authority. 11 In him also you were circumcised with a circumcision made without hands, by putting off the body of the flesh, by the circumcision of Christ, 12 having been buried with him in baptism, in which you were also raised with him through faith in the powerful working of God, who raised him from the dead. 13 And you, who were dead in your trespasses and the uncircumcision of your flesh, God made alive together with him, having forgiven us all our trespasses, 14 by canceling the record of debt that stood against us with its legal demands. This he set aside, nailing it to the cross. 15 He disarmed the rulers and authorities and put them to open shame, by triumphing over them in him.

The rest of chapter 2 focuses on Paul's deep concerns about the false teaching being promoted in the Colossian church.

1. What are the "elemental spirits" urging the Christians in Colossae to do (v. 8)?

2. What does Paul want them to remember instead (vv. 9-15)? How will this affect their attitude towards those "elemental spirits"?

3. The false teachers urged the Colossians to observe certain religious practices as a way of progressing spiritually (e.g. circumcision and legalism—both of which Paul counters in verses 12-15). What are some modern equivalents?

4. Do Paul's solutions still stand? Why?

PONDER Jesus cancelled the "record of debt" that stood against you (v. 14; cf. Eph 2:14-16[44]). What impact has this had on you?

PRAYER IDEAS Ask God to help you to continue to walk in Christ, rooted and built up in him (vv. 6-7).

READING 51   COLOSSIANS 2:15-23

He disarmed the rulers and authorities and put them to open shame, by triumphing over them in him.
¹⁶ Therefore let no one pass judgment on you in questions of food and drink, or with regard to a festival or a new moon or a Sabbath. ¹⁷ These are a shadow of the things to come, but the substance belongs to Christ. ¹⁸ Let no one disqualify you, insisting on asceticism and worship of angels, going on in detail about visions, puffed up without reason by his sensuous mind, ¹⁹ and not holding fast to the Head, from whom the whole body, nourished and knit together through its joints and ligaments, grows with a growth that is from God.
²⁰ If with Christ you died to the elemental spirits of the world, why, as if you were still alive in the world, do you submit to regulations— ²¹ "Do not handle, Do not taste, Do not touch" ²² (referring to things that all perish as they are used)—according to human precepts and teachings? ²³ These have indeed an appearance of wisdom in promoting self-made religion and asceticism and severity to the body, but they are of no value in stopping the indulgence of the flesh.

1. What are the two things Paul commands the Colossians to do in verses 16-19?

2. What things does Paul reject in this passage? Why?

---

44. For he himself is our peace, who has made us both one and has broken down in his flesh the dividing wall of hostility ¹⁵ by abolishing the law of commandments expressed in ordinances, that he might create in himself one new man in place of the two, so making peace, ¹⁶ and might reconcile us both to God in one body through the cross, thereby killing the hostility.

3. In this section and the previous one (vv. 6-15—see Reading 50), Paul keeps coming back to Jesus again and again. What aspects of Jesus' life and work does he focus on?

PONDER Why is it helpful to have this constant focus on Jesus and his work?

PRAYER IDEAS Thank God for all that the book of Colossians has taught you about Jesus so far. Thank God for the ways Jesus has changed you since you became a Christian.

READING 52 — COLOSSIANS 3:1-4

If then you have been raised with Christ, seek the things that are above, where Christ is, seated at the right hand of God. 2 Set your minds on things that are above, not on things that are on earth. 3 For you have died, and your life is hidden with Christ in God. 4 When Christ who is your life appears, then you also will appear with him in glory.

Paul makes some important statements about the Colossians and where they stand with God: some things happened decisively in the past, some are present realities and some lie in the future.

1. What does Paul say about your past, present and future (vv. 1-4)?

2. In the light of these facts, what does Paul instruct the Colossians to do (v. 2)?

3. What do you think Paul means by "things that are above" and "things that are on earth" (v. 2)?

PONDER How does the promise of verse 4 affect your life now?

PRAYER IDEAS Ask God to help you to set your mind on "things that are above" (v. 2).

READING 53 — COLOSSIANS 3:5-11

Put to death therefore what is earthly in you: sexual immorality, impurity, passion, evil desire, and covetousness, which is idolatry. 6 On account of these the wrath of God is coming. 7 In these you too once walked, when you were living in them. 8 But now you must put them all away: anger, wrath, malice, slander, and obscene talk from your mouth. 9 Do not lie to one another, seeing that you have put off the old self with its practices 10 and have put on the new self, which is being renewed in knowledge after the image of its creator. 11 Here there is not Greek and Jew, circumcised and uncircumcised, barbarian, Scythian, slave, free; but Christ is all, and in all.

1. What is the down-to-earth result of the

heavenly mindedness spoken of in the last reading (vv. 5-10)?

2. What are the reasons Paul gives for why you should get rid of these behaviours? Are they incentives for you to change?

3. Which of these behaviours do you find particularly challenging to 'put to death'?

PONDER Why do you think Paul used such strong expressions like 'put to death' (v. 5)?

PRAYER IDEAS Ask God to give you the strength and conviction to put these things to death in your life.

READING 54 — COLOSSIANS 3:12-17

Put on then, as God's chosen ones, holy and beloved, compassionate hearts, kindness, humility, meekness, and patience, 13 bearing with one another and, if one has a complaint against another, forgiving each other; as the Lord has forgiven you, so you also must forgive. 14 And above all these put on love, which binds everything together in perfect harmony. 15 And let the peace of Christ rule in your hearts, to which indeed you were called in one body. And be thankful. 16 Let the word of Christ dwell in you richly, teaching and admonishing one another in all wisdom, singing psalms and hymns and spiritual songs, with thankfulness in your hearts to God. 17 And whatever you do, in word or deed, do everything in the name of the Lord Jesus, giving thanks to God the Father through him.

1. How does Paul describe the Colossian Christians in verse 12? What is the significance of this (cf. Deut 7:6[45])?

2. Paul has already talked about what you should 'put off'; now he talks about what you should 'put on'. What are the things Paul says you should clothe yourself with?

3. Which ones are the most difficult for you to 'put on'?

PONDER Which things in Paul's list do you need to work on? What can you do to cultivate these things?

PRAYER IDEAS Ask God to give you the conviction and commitment to 'put on' these things in your life.

---

45. "For you are a people holy to the LORD your God. The LORD your God has chosen you to be a people for his treasured possession, out of all the peoples who are on the face of the earth."

READING 55 — COLOSSIANS 3:12-17

Put on then, as God's chosen ones, holy and beloved, compassionate hearts, kindness, humility, meekness, and patience, 13 bearing with one another and, if one has a complaint against another, forgiving each other; as the Lord has forgiven you, so you also must forgive. 14 And above all these put on love, which binds everything together in perfect harmony. 15 And let the peace of Christ rule in your hearts, to which indeed you were called in one body. And be thankful. 16 Let the word of Christ dwell in you richly, teaching and admonishing one another in all wisdom, singing psalms and hymns and spiritual songs, with thankfulness in your hearts to God. 17 And whatever you do, in word or deed, do everything in the name of the Lord Jesus, giving thanks to God the Father through him.

1. Looking back at the end of chapter 2, Paul argued against those who say "You must obey this rule and keep that law if you want to be a real Christian". What is the difference between what Paul is doing in this section and what the false teachers were saying?

2. How should love be expressed in their community (vv. 13-14)?

3. What are some practical examples of how to "do everything in the name of the Lord Jesus" (v. 17)?

PONDER How can you let "the word of Christ dwell in you richly" (v. 16)?

PRAYER IDEAS Ask God to help you love the people in your church the way Paul encourages you to.

READING 56 — COLOSSIANS 3:18-4:1

Wives, submit to your husbands, as is fitting in the Lord. 19 Husbands, love your wives, and do not be harsh with them. 20 Children, obey your parents in everything, for this pleases the Lord. 21 Fathers, do not provoke your children, lest they become discouraged. 22 Slaves, obey in everything those who are your earthly masters, not by way of eye-service, as people-pleasers, but with sincerity of heart, fearing the Lord. 23 Whatever you do, work heartily, as for the Lord and not for men, 24 knowing that from the Lord you will receive the inheritance as your reward. You are serving the Lord Christ. 25 For the wrongdoer will be paid back for the wrong he has done, and there is no partiality.

4:1 Masters, treat your slaves justly and fairly, knowing that you also have a Master in heaven.

1. List the commands Paul gives to:

   a) husbands and wives

   b) children and parents

   c) slaves and masters.

2. What is the responsibility of a Christian wife (v. 18)? Why is this "fitting in the Lord"?

3. How are Christian husbands to love their wives (cf. Eph 5:25-33[46])?

PONDER What do you like/dislike/struggle with about the roles and responsibilities of husbands and wives outlined by Paul?

PRAYER IDEAS Ask God to help you to honour him in all of your relationships.

READING 57 — COLOSSIANS 3:18-4:1

Wives, submit to your husbands, as is fitting in the Lord. [19] Husbands, love your wives, and do not be harsh with them. [20] Children, obey your parents in everything, for this pleases the Lord. [21] Fathers, do not provoke your children, lest they become discouraged. [22] Slaves, obey in everything those who are your earthly masters, not by way of eye-service, as people-pleasers, but with sincerity of heart, fearing the Lord. [23] Whatever you do, work heartily, as for the Lord and not for men, [24] knowing that from the Lord you will receive the inheritance as your reward. You are serving the Lord Christ. [25] For the wrongdoer will be paid back for the wrong he has done, and there is no partiality.
4:1 Masters, treat your slaves justly and fairly, knowing that you also have a Master in heaven.

1. Compare Colossians 3:18-19 with Galatians 3:28.[47] Has Paul contradicted himself, or are his instructions to husbands and wives in Colossians consistent with his teaching in Galatians regarding sexual equality? Why/why not?

2. How do parents (fathers especially) provoke their children?

3. How do the principles Paul outlines in 3:22-4:1 apply to your work situation?

---

46. Husbands, love your wives, as Christ loved the church and gave himself up for her, [26] that he might sanctify her, having cleansed her by the washing of water with the word, [27] so that he might present the church to himself in splendor, without spot or wrinkle or any such thing, that she might be holy and without blemish. [28] In the same way husbands should love their wives as their own bodies. He who loves his wife loves himself. [29] For no one ever hated his own flesh, but nourishes and cherishes it, just as Christ does the church, [30] because we are members of his body. [31] "Therefore a man shall leave his father and mother and hold fast to his wife, and the two shall become one flesh." [32] This mystery is profound, and I am saying that it refers to Christ and the church. [33] However, let each one of you love his wife as himself, and let the wife see that she respects her husband.
47. There is neither Jew nor Greek, there is neither slave nor free, there is no male and female, for you are all one in Christ Jesus.

PONDER How can you better serve each member of your family?

PRAYER IDEAS Thank God for the opportunities he gives you to serve the members of your family.

READING 58 — COLOSSIANS 4:2-6

Continue steadfastly in prayer, being watchful in it with thanksgiving. 3 At the same time, pray also for us, that God may open to us a door for the word, to declare the mystery of Christ, on account of which I am in prison— 4 that I may make it clear, which is how I ought to speak.

5 Walk in wisdom toward outsiders, making the best use of the time. 6 Let your speech always be gracious, seasoned with salt, so that you may know how you ought to answer each person.

1. Looking at verses 3-4, what is Paul's responsibility in evangelism?

2. What are the Colossians' responsibilities in evangelism (vv. 2, 5-6)?

3. How might you "[w]alk in wisdom toward outsiders"? How can you make "the best use of the time" (v. 5)?

PONDER What would it mean for your conversation to be "gracious, seasoned with salt" (v. 6)?

PRAYER IDEAS Ask God to give you opportunities to share your faith. Ask him to help you to make your conversations more gracious and 'salty'.

READING 59 — COLOSSIANS 4:2-18

Continue steadfastly in prayer, being watchful in it with thanksgiving. 3 At the same time, pray also for us, that God may open to us a door for the word, to declare the mystery of Christ, on account of which I am in prison— 4 that I may make it clear, which is how I ought to speak.

5 Walk in wisdom toward outsiders, making the best use of the time. 6 Let your speech always be gracious, seasoned with salt, so that you may know how you ought to answer each person.

7 Tychicus will tell you all about my activities. He is a beloved brother and faithful minister and fellow servant in the Lord. 8 I have sent him to you for this very purpose, that you may know how we are and that he may encourage your hearts, 9 and with him Onesimus, our faithful and beloved brother, who is one of you. They will tell you of everything that has taken place here.

10 Aristarchus my fellow prisoner greets you, and Mark the cousin of Barnabas (concerning whom you have received instructions—if he comes to you, welcome him), 11 and Jesus who is called Justus. These are the only men of the circumcision among my fellow workers for the kingdom of God, and they have

been a comfort to me. [12] Epaphras, who is one of you, a servant of Christ Jesus, greets you, always struggling on your behalf in his prayers, that you may stand mature and fully assured in all the will of God. [13] For I bear him witness that he has worked hard for you and for those in Laodicea and in Hierapolis. [14] Luke the beloved physician greets you, as does Demas. [15] Give my greetings to the brothers at Laodicea, and to Nympha and the church in her house. [16] And when this letter has been read among you, have it also read in the church of the Laodiceans; and see that you also read the letter from Laodicea. [17] And say to Archippus, "See that you fulfill the ministry that you have received in the Lord."

[18] I, Paul, write this greeting with my own hand. Remember my chains. Grace be with you.

1. Paul urges the Colossians to be watchful and thankful (v. 2). What are they to be watchful and thankful for? (Hint: remember the context by looking back at 3:1-4.[48])

2. What does this passage teach you about the nature of prayer (vv. 2, 12-13)?

3. What does this passage teach you about the content of prayer (vv. 3-4, 12)?

PONDER How would you describe your prayer life? How does it compare to Epaphras'?

PRAYER IDEAS Ask God to help you to make prayer a priority.

READING 60   COLOSSIANS 4:7-18

Tychicus will tell you all about my activities. He is a beloved brother and faithful minister and fellow servant in the Lord. [8] I have sent him to you for this very purpose, that you may know how we are and that he may encourage your hearts, [9] and with him Onesimus, our faithful and beloved brother, who is one of you. They will tell you of everything that has taken place here.

[10] Aristarchus my fellow prisoner greets you, and Mark the cousin of Barnabas (concerning whom you have received instructions—if he comes to you, welcome him), [11] and Jesus who is called Justus. These are the only men of the circumcision among my fellow workers for the kingdom of God, and they have been a comfort to me. [12] Epaphras, who is one of you, a servant of Christ Jesus, greets you, always struggling on your behalf in his prayers, that you may stand mature and fully assured in all the will of God. [13] For I bear him witness that he has worked hard for you and for those in Laodicea and in Hierapolis. [14] Luke the beloved physician greets you, as does Demas. [15] Give my greetings to the brothers at Laodicea, and to Nympha and the church in her house. [16] And when this letter has been read among you, have it also read in the church of the Laodiceans; and see that you also read the letter from Laodicea. [17] And say to Archippus, "See that you fulfill the ministry that you

---

48. If then you have been raised with Christ, seek the things that are above, where Christ is, seated at the right hand of God. [2] Set your minds on things that are above, not on things that are on earth. [3] For you have died, and your life is hidden with Christ in God. [4] When Christ who is your life appears, then you also will appear with him in glory.

have received in the Lord."

¹⁸ I, Paul, write this greeting with my own hand. Remember my chains. Grace be with you.

1. What do you learn about each of the individuals Paul mentions in his final greeting?

2. How does their example reinforce the teaching of his letter?

3. Much of this last section is about encouraging the Christians in Colossae. How do you give and receive encouragement?

4. Why do you think Paul ends this letter with "Remember my chains" (v. 18)?

PONDER What do you think it means to 'struggle' on behalf of someone else in prayer (v. 12)?

PRAYER IDEAS Thank God for the people who encourage you in your Christian life. Ask him to give you opportunities to do likewise to others.

APPENDIX

ADDITIONAL PASSAGES REFERRED TO ...

Psalm 2 (Reading 9)

Why do the nations rage
and the peoples plot in vain?
[2] The kings of the earth set themselves,
and the rulers take counsel together,
against the Lord and against his
Anointed, saying,
[3] "Let us burst their bonds apart
and cast away their cords from us."

[4] He who sits in the heavens laughs;
the Lord holds them in derision.
[5] Then he will speak to them in his wrath,
and terrify them in his fury, saying,
[6] "As for me, I have set my King
on Zion, my holy hill."

[7] I will tell of the decree:
The Lord said to me, "You are my Son;
today I have begotten you.
[8] Ask of me, and I will make the nations
your heritage,
and the ends of the earth your
possession.
[9] You shall break them with a rod of iron
and dash them in pieces like a potter's
vessel."

[10] Now therefore, O kings, be wise;
be warned, O rulers of the earth.
[11] Serve the Lord with fear,
and rejoice with trembling.
[12] Kiss the Son,
lest he be angry, and you perish in the
way,
for his wrath is quickly kindled.
Blessed are all who take refuge in him.

Galatians 3:7-29 (Reading 14)

Know then that it is those of faith who are the sons of Abraham. [8] And the Scripture, foreseeing that God would justify the Gentiles by faith, preached the gospel beforehand to Abraham, saying, "In you shall all the nations be blessed." [9] So then, those who are of faith are blessed along with Abraham, the man of faith.

[10] For all who rely on works of the law are under a curse; for it is written, "Cursed be everyone who does not abide by all things written in the Book of the Law, and do them." [11] Now it is evident that no one is justified before God by the law, for "The righteous shall live by faith." [12] But the law is not of faith, rather "The one who does them shall live by them." [13] Christ redeemed us from the curse of the law by becoming a curse for us—for it is written, "Cursed is everyone who is hanged on a tree"— [14] so that in Christ Jesus the blessing of Abraham might come to the Gentiles, so that we might receive the promised Spirit through faith.

[15] To give a human example, brothers: even with a man-made covenant, no one annuls it or adds to it once it has been ratified. [16] Now the promises were made to Abraham and to his offspring. It does not say, "And to offsprings," referring to many, but referring to one, "And to your offspring," who is Christ. [17] This is what I mean: the law, which came 430 years afterward, does not annul a covenant previously ratified by God, so as to make the promise void. [18] For if the inheritance comes by the law, it no longer comes by promise; but God gave it to Abraham by a promise.

¹⁹ Why then the law? It was added because of transgressions, until the offspring should come to whom the promise had been made, and it was put in place through angels by an intermediary. ²⁰ Now an intermediary implies more than one, but God is one.

²¹ Is the law then contrary to the promises of God? Certainly not! For if a law had been given that could give life, then righteousness would indeed be by the law. ²² But the Scripture imprisoned everything under sin, so that the promise by faith in Jesus Christ might be given to those who believe.

²³ Now before faith came, we were held captive under the law, imprisoned until the coming faith would be revealed. ²⁴ So then, the law was our guardian until Christ came, in order that we might be justified by faith. ²⁵ But now that faith has come, we are no longer under a guardian, ²⁶ for in Christ Jesus you are all sons of God, through faith. ²⁷ For as many of you as were baptized into Christ have put on Christ. ²⁸ There is neither Jew nor Greek, there is neither slave nor free, there is no male and female, for you are all one in Christ Jesus. ²⁹ And if you are Christ's, then you are Abraham's offspring, heirs according to promise.

1 Corinthians 15:1-11 (Reading 18)

Now I would remind you, brothers, of the gospel I preached to you, which you received, in which you stand, ² and by which you are being saved, if you hold fast to the word I preached to you—unless you believed in vain.

³ For I delivered to you as of first importance what I also received: that Christ died for our sins in accordance with the Scriptures, ⁴ that he was buried, that he was raised on the third day in accordance with the Scriptures, ⁵ and that he appeared to Cephas, then to the twelve. ⁶ Then he appeared to more than five hundred brothers at one time, most of whom are still alive, though some have fallen asleep. ⁷ Then he appeared to James, then to all the apostles. ⁸ Last of all, as to one untimely born, he appeared also to me. ⁹ For I am the least of the apostles, unworthy to be called an apostle, because I persecuted the church of God. ¹⁰ But by the grace of God I am what I am, and his grace toward me was not in vain. On the contrary, I worked harder than any of them, though it was not I, but the grace of God that is with me. ¹¹ Whether then it was I or they, so we preach and so you believed.

Galatians 1:11-24 (Reading 19)

For I would have you know, brothers, that the gospel that was preached by me is not man's gospel. ¹² For I did not receive it from any man, nor was I taught it, but I received it through a revelation of Jesus Christ. ¹³ For you have heard of my former life in Judaism, how I persecuted the church of God violently and tried to destroy it. ¹⁴ And I was advancing in Judaism beyond many of my own age among my people, so extremely zealous was I for the traditions of my fathers. ¹⁵ But when he who had set me apart before I was born, and who called me by his grace, ¹⁶ was pleased to reveal his Son to me, in order that I might preach him among the Gentiles, I did not immediately consult with anyone; ¹⁷ nor did I go up to Jerusalem to those who were apostles before me, but I went away into Arabia, and returned again to Damascus.

¹⁸ Then after three years I went up to Jerusalem to visit Cephas and remained with him fifteen days. ¹⁹ But I saw none of the other apostles except James the Lord's brother. ²⁰ (In what I am writing to you, before God, I do not lie!) ²¹ Then I went into the regions of Syria and Cilicia. ²² And I was still unknown in person to the churches of Judea that are in Christ. ²³ They only were hearing it said, "He who used to persecute us is now preaching the faith he once tried to destroy." ²⁴ And they glorified God because of me.

Exodus 12 (Reading 22 and 25)

The LORD said to Moses and Aaron in the land of Egypt, 2 "This month shall be for you the beginning of months. It shall be the first month of the year for you. 3 Tell all the congregation of Israel that on the tenth day of this month every man shall take a lamb according to their fathers' houses, a lamb for a household. 4 And if the household is too small for a lamb, then he and his nearest neighbor shall take according to the number of persons; according to what each can eat you shall make your count for the lamb. 5 Your lamb shall be without blemish, a male a year old. You may take it from the sheep or from the goats, 6 and you shall keep it until the fourteenth day of this month, when the whole assembly of the congregation of Israel shall kill their lambs at twilight.

7 "Then they shall take some of the blood and put it on the two doorposts and the lintel of the houses in which they eat it. 8 They shall eat the flesh that night, roasted on the fire; with unleavened bread and bitter herbs they shall eat it. 9 Do not eat any of it raw or boiled in water, but roasted, its head with its legs and its inner parts. 10 And you shall let none of it remain until the morning; anything that remains until the morning you shall burn. 11 In this manner you shall eat it: with your belt fastened, your sandals on your feet, and your staff in your hand. And you shall eat it in haste. It is the LORD's Passover. 12 For I will pass through the land of Egypt that night, and I will strike all the firstborn in the land of Egypt, both man and beast; and on all the gods of Egypt I will execute judgments: I am the LORD. 13 The blood shall be a sign for you, on the houses where you are. And when I see the blood, I will pass over you, and no plague will befall you to destroy you, when I strike the land of Egypt.

14 "This day shall be for you a memorial day, and you shall keep it as a feast to the LORD; throughout your generations, as a statute forever, you shall keep it as a feast. 15 Seven days you shall eat unleavened bread. On the first day you shall remove leaven out of your houses, for if anyone eats what is leavened, from the first day until the seventh day, that person shall be cut off from Israel. 16 On the first day you shall hold a holy assembly, and on the seventh day a holy assembly. No work shall be done on those days. But what everyone needs to eat, that alone may be prepared by you. 17 And you shall observe the Feast of Unleavened Bread, for on this very day I brought your hosts out of the land of Egypt. Therefore you shall observe this day, throughout your generations, as a statute forever. 18 In the first month, from the fourteenth day of the month at evening, you shall eat unleavened bread until the twenty-first day of the month at evening. 19 For seven days no leaven is to be found in your houses. If anyone eats what is leavened, that person will be cut off from the congregation of Israel, whether he is a sojourner or a native of the land. 20 You shall eat nothing leavened; in all your dwelling places you shall eat unleavened bread."

21 Then Moses called all the elders of Israel and said to them, "Go and select lambs for yourselves according to your clans, and kill the Passover lamb. 22 Take a bunch of hyssop and dip it in the blood that is in the basin, and touch the lintel and the two doorposts with the blood that is in the basin. None of you shall go out of the door of his house until the morning. 23 For the LORD will pass through to strike the Egyptians, and when he sees the blood on the lintel and on the two doorposts, the LORD will pass over the door and will not allow the destroyer to enter your houses to strike you. 24 You shall observe this rite as a statute for you and for your sons forever. 25 And when you come to the land that the LORD will give you, as he has promised, you shall keep this service. 26 And when your children say to you, 'What do you mean by this service?' 27 you shall say, 'It is the sacrifice of the LORD's Passover, for he passed over

the houses of the people of Israel in Egypt, when he struck the Egyptians but spared our houses.'" And the people bowed their heads and worshiped.

28 Then the people of Israel went and did so; as the Lord had commanded Moses and Aaron, so they did.

29 At midnight the Lord struck down all the firstborn in the land of Egypt, from the firstborn of Pharaoh who sat on his throne to the firstborn of the captive who was in the dungeon, and all the firstborn of the livestock. 30 And Pharaoh rose up in the night, he and all his servants and all the Egyptians. And there was a great cry in Egypt, for there was not a house where someone was not dead. 31 Then he summoned Moses and Aaron by night and said, "Up, go out from among my people, both you and the people of Israel; and go, serve the Lord, as you have said. 32 Take your flocks and your herds, as you have said, and be gone, and bless me also!"

33 The Egyptians were urgent with the people to send them out of the land in haste. For they said, "We shall all be dead." 34 So the people took their dough before it was leavened, their kneading bowls being bound up in their cloaks on their shoulders. 35 The people of Israel had also done as Moses told them, for they had asked the Egyptians for silver and gold jewelry and for clothing. 36 And the Lord had given the people favor in the sight of the Egyptians, so that they let them have what they asked. Thus they plundered the Egyptians.

37 And the people of Israel journeyed from Rameses to Succoth, about six hundred thousand men on foot, besides women and children. 38 A mixed multitude also went up with them, and very much livestock, both flocks and herds. 39 And they baked unleavened cakes of the dough that they had brought out of Egypt, for it was not leavened, because they were thrust out of Egypt and could not wait, nor had they prepared any provisions for themselves.

40 The time that the people of Israel lived in Egypt was 430 years. 41 At the end of 430 years, on that very day, all the hosts of the Lord went out from the land of Egypt. 42 It was a night of watching by the Lord, to bring them out of the land of Egypt; so this same night is a night of watching kept to the Lord by all the people of Israel throughout their generations.

43 And the Lord said to Moses and Aaron, "This is the statute of the Passover: no foreigner shall eat of it, 44 but every slave that is bought for money may eat of it after you have circumcised him. 45 No foreigner or hired servant may eat of it. 46 It shall be eaten in one house; you shall not take any of the flesh outside the house, and you shall not break any of its bones. 47 All the congregation of Israel shall keep it. 48 If a stranger shall sojourn with you and would keep the Passover to the Lord, let all his males be circumcised. Then he may come near and keep it; he shall be as a native of the land. But no uncircumcised person shall eat of it. 49 There shall be one law for the native and for the stranger who sojourns among you."

50 All the people of Israel did just as the Lord commanded Moses and Aaron. 51 And on that very day the Lord brought the people of Israel out of the land of Egypt by their hosts.

1 Corinthians 10:1-13 (Reading 28)

For I want you to know, brothers, that our fathers were all under the cloud, and all passed through the sea, 2 and all were baptized into Moses in the cloud and in the sea, 3 and all ate the same spiritual food, 4 and all drank the same spiritual drink. For they drank from the spiritual Rock that followed them, and the Rock was Christ. 5 Nevertheless, with most of them God was not pleased, for they were overthrown in the wilderness.

6 Now these things took place as examples for us, that we might not desire evil as they did. 7 Do not be idolaters as some of them were; as it is written, "The people sat down to

eat and drink and rose up to play." [8] We must not indulge in sexual immorality as some of them did, and twenty-three thousand fell in a single day. [9] We must not put Christ to the test, as some of them did and were destroyed by serpents, [10] nor grumble, as some of them did and were destroyed by the Destroyer. [11] Now these things happened to them as an example, but they were written down for our instruction, on whom the end of the ages has come. [12] Therefore let anyone who thinks that he stands take heed lest he fall. [13] No temptation has overtaken you that is not common to man. God is faithful, and he will not let you be tempted beyond your ability, but with the temptation he will also provide the way of escape, that you may be able to endure it.

Numbers 20:2-13 (Reading 35)

Now there was no water for the congregation. And they assembled themselves together against Moses and against Aaron. [3] And the people quarreled with Moses and said, "Would that we had perished when our brothers perished before the Lord! [4] Why have you brought the assembly of the Lord into this wilderness, that we should die here, both we and our cattle? [5] And why have you made us come up out of Egypt to bring us to this evil place? It is no place for grain or figs or vines or pomegranates, and there is no water to drink." [6] Then Moses and Aaron went from the presence of the assembly to the entrance of the tent of meeting and fell on their faces. And the glory of the Lord appeared to them, [7] and the Lord spoke to Moses, saying, [8] "Take the staff, and assemble the congregation, you and Aaron your brother, and tell the rock before their eyes to yield its water. So you shall bring water out of the rock for them and give drink to the congregation and their cattle." [9] And Moses took the staff from before the Lord, as he commanded him.

[10] Then Moses and Aaron gathered the assembly together before the rock, and he said to them, "Hear now, you rebels: shall we bring water for you out of this rock?" [11] And Moses lifted up his hand and struck the rock with his staff twice, and water came out abundantly, and the congregation drank, and their livestock. [12] And the Lord said to Moses and Aaron, "Because you did not believe in me, to uphold me as holy in the eyes of the people of Israel, therefore you shall not bring this assembly into the land that I have given them." [13] These are the waters of Meribah, where the people of Israel quarreled with the Lord, and through them he showed himself holy.

Leviticus 25 (Reading 39)

The Lord spoke to Moses on Mount Sinai, saying, [2] "Speak to the people of Israel and say to them, When you come into the land that I give you, the land shall keep a Sabbath to the Lord. [3] For six years you shall sow your field, and for six years you shall prune your vineyard and gather in its fruits, [4] but in the seventh year there shall be a Sabbath of solemn rest for the land, a Sabbath to the Lord. You shall not sow your field or prune your vineyard. [5] You shall not reap what grows of itself in your harvest, or gather the grapes of your undressed vine. It shall be a year of solemn rest for the land. [6] The Sabbath of the land shall provide food for you, for yourself and for your male and female slaves and for your hired servant and the sojourner who lives with you, [7] and for your cattle and for the wild animals that are in your land: all its yield shall be for food.

[8] "You shall count seven weeks of years, seven times seven years, so that the time of the seven weeks of years shall give you forty-nine years. [9] Then you shall sound the loud trumpet on the tenth day of the seventh month. On the Day of Atonement you shall sound the trumpet throughout all your land. [10] And you shall consecrate the fiftieth year, and proclaim liberty throughout the land

to all its inhabitants. It shall be a jubilee for you, when each of you shall return to his property and each of you shall return to his clan. ¹¹ That fiftieth year shall be a jubilee for you; in it you shall neither sow nor reap what grows of itself nor gather the grapes from the undressed vines. ¹² For it is a jubilee. It shall be holy to you. You may eat the produce of the field.

¹³ "In this year of jubilee each of you shall return to his property. ¹⁴ And if you make a sale to your neighbor or buy from your neighbor, you shall not wrong one another. ¹⁵ You shall pay your neighbor according to the number of years after the jubilee, and he shall sell to you according to the number of years for crops. ¹⁶ If the years are many, you shall increase the price, and if the years are few, you shall reduce the price, for it is the number of the crops that he is selling to you. ¹⁷ You shall not wrong one another, but you shall fear your God, for I am the Lord your God.

¹⁸ "Therefore you shall do my statutes and keep my rules and perform them, and then you will dwell in the land securely. ¹⁹ The land will yield its fruit, and you will eat your fill and dwell in it securely. ²⁰ And if you say, 'What shall we eat in the seventh year, if we may not sow or gather in our crop?' ²¹ I will command my blessing on you in the sixth year, so that it will produce a crop sufficient for three years. ²² When you sow in the eighth year, you will be eating some of the old crop; you shall eat the old until the ninth year, when its crop arrives.

²³ "The land shall not be sold in perpetuity, for the land is mine. For you are strangers and sojourners with me. ²⁴ And in all the country you possess, you shall allow a redemption of the land.

²⁵ "If your brother becomes poor and sells part of his property, then his nearest redeemer shall come and redeem what his brother has sold. ²⁶ If a man has no one to redeem it and then himself becomes prosperous and finds sufficient means to redeem it, ²⁷ let him calculate the years since he sold it and pay back the balance to the man to whom he sold it, and then return to his property. ²⁸ But if he has not sufficient means to recover it, then what he sold shall remain in the hand of the buyer until the year of jubilee. In the jubilee it shall be released, and he shall return to his property.

²⁹ "If a man sells a dwelling house in a walled city, he may redeem it within a year of its sale. For a full year he shall have the right of redemption. ³⁰ If it is not redeemed within a full year, then the house in the walled city shall belong in perpetuity to the buyer, throughout his generations; it shall not be released in the jubilee. ³¹ But the houses of the villages that have no wall around them shall be classified with the fields of the land. They may be redeemed, and they shall be released in the jubilee. ³² As for the cities of the Levites, the Levites may redeem at any time the houses in the cities they possess. ³³ And if one of the Levites exercises his right of redemption, then the house that was sold in a city they possess shall be released in the jubilee. For the houses in the cities of the Levites are their possession among the people of Israel. ³⁴ But the fields of pastureland belonging to their cities may not be sold, for that is their possession forever.

³⁵ "If your brother becomes poor and cannot maintain himself with you, you shall support him as though he were a stranger and a sojourner, and he shall live with you. ³⁶ Take no interest from him or profit, but fear your God, that your brother may live beside you. ³⁷ You shall not lend him your money at interest, nor give him your food for profit. ³⁸ I am the Lord your God, who brought you out of the land of Egypt to give you the land of Canaan, and to be your God.

³⁹ "If your brother becomes poor beside you and sells himself to you, you shall not make him serve as a slave: ⁴⁰ he shall be with you as a hired servant and as a sojourner.

He shall serve with you until the year of the jubilee. ⁴¹ Then he shall go out from you, he and his children with him, and go back to his own clan and return to the possession of his fathers. ⁴² For they are my servants, whom I brought out of the land of Egypt; they shall not be sold as slaves. ⁴³ You shall not rule over him ruthlessly but shall fear your God. ⁴⁴ As for your male and female slaves whom you may have: you may buy male and female slaves from among the nations that are around you. ⁴⁵ You may also buy from among the strangers who sojourn with you and their clans that are with you, who have been born in your land, and they may be your property. ⁴⁶ You may bequeath them to your sons after you to inherit as a possession forever. You may make slaves of them, but over your brothers the people of Israel you shall not rule, one over another ruthlessly.

⁴⁷ "If a stranger or sojourner with you becomes rich, and your brother beside him becomes poor and sells himself to the stranger or sojourner with you or to a member of the stranger's clan, ⁴⁸ then after he is sold he may be redeemed. One of his brothers may redeem him, ⁴⁹ or his uncle or his cousin may redeem him, or a close relative from his clan may redeem him. Or if he grows rich he may redeem himself. ⁵⁰ He shall calculate with his buyer from the year when he sold himself to him until the year of jubilee, and the price of his sale shall vary with the number of years. The time he was with his owner shall be rated as the time of a hired servant. ⁵¹ If there are still many years left, he shall pay proportionately for his redemption some of his sale price. ⁵² If there remain but a few years until the year of jubilee, he shall calculate and pay for his redemption in proportion to his years of service. ⁵³ He shall treat him as a servant hired year by year. He shall not rule ruthlessly over him in your sight. ⁵⁴ And if he is not redeemed by these means, then he and his children with him shall be released in the year of jubilee. ⁵⁵ For it is to me that the people of Israel are servants. They are my servants whom I brought out of the land of Egypt: I am the LORD your God."

Feedback on this resource

We really appreciate getting feedback about our resources—not just suggestions for how to improve them, but also positive feedback and ways they can be used. We especially love to hear that the resources may have helped someone in their Christian growth.

You can send feedback to us via the 'Feedback' menu in our online store, or write to us at PO Box 225, Kingsford NSW 2032, Australia.

matthiasmedia

Matthias Media is an evangelical publishing ministry that seeks to persuade all Christians of the Bible-shaped, theological truth of God's purposes in Jesus Christ, and equip them with high-quality resources, so that they will:

- abandon their lives to the honour and service of Christ in daily holiness and decision-making
- pray constantly in Christ's name for the growth of his gospel
- speak the Bible's life-changing word whenever and however they can—in the home, in the world and in the fellowship of his people.

It was in 1988 that we first started pursuing this mission, and in God's kindness we now have more than 300 different ministry resources being used all over the world. These resources range from Bible studies and books through to training courses and audio sermons.

To find out more about our large range of very useful resources, and to access samples and free downloads, visit our website:

www.matthiasmedia.com.au

How to buy our resources

1. Direct from us over the internet:
   - in the US: www.matthiasmedia.com
   - in Australia and the rest of the world: www.matthiasmedia.com.au

2. Direct from us by phone:
   - in the US: 1 866 407 4530
   - in Australia: 1800 814 360 (Sydney: 9663 1478)
   - international: +61-2-9663-1478

3. Through a range of outlets in various parts of the world. Visit **www.matthiasmedia.com.au/international.php** for details about recommended retailers in your part of the world, including www.thegoodbook.co.uk in the United Kingdom.

4. Trade enquiries can be addressed to:
   - in the US and Canada: sales@matthiasmedia.com
   - in Australia and the rest of the world: sales@matthiasmedia.com.au

> Register at our website for our **free** regular email update to receive information about the latest new resources, **exclusive special offers**, and free articles to help you grow in your Christian life and ministry.

THE ESV BIBLE

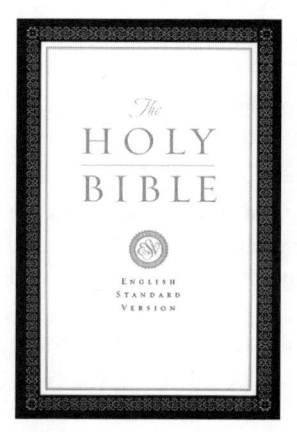

Since its much-anticipated release in late 2001, the English Standard Version (ESV) Bible has won increasing acceptance in churches throughout the US, England and Australia as an accurate, readable Bible for general use.

The secret of the ESV's success has been its ability to balance two crucial factors in Bible translation. On the one hand, it seeks to be an 'essentially literal' translation, retaining some of the form and flavour of the ancient text, and sticking as closely as possible to its thought-forms and imagery. At the same time, the ESV strives to be flowing and readable for a modern audience.

This balancing act is never possible to achieve perfectly, but the ESV is thought by many to do the best job of any English translation currently available.

This makes it suitable for a wide variety of purposes, including public reading and preaching, private and small group study, memorization, and so on.

"The English Standard Version is noticeably better than the current most popular English translations of the Bible. The ESV brings us closer to what the authors actually wrote, and therefore what the Author actually says. Bible readers, teachers and preachers: this is the translation we have been waiting for, contemporary but more precisely accurate."

Rev. Dr John Woodhouse
Principal, Moore College, Sydney

To find out more about the ESV, and to view online samples, go to
www.matthiasmedia.com.au/ESV